BOL MAYWAL

A Mother's Promise

A Civil War Survivor and Her Pursuit of the American Dream

FOR Mr. Patrick Eakes,

Thank you for your dedication, leadership, and service to the community, and the Rotary family. Continue your selfless service.

B. Maywal

BOL MAYWAL
Rotary Peace Fellow.
Nov. 8, 2024

SPARK Publications
Charlotte, North Carolina

A Mother's Promise: A Civil War Survivor and Her Pursuit of the American Dream
Bol Maywal

Designed, produced, and published by SPARK Publications
SPARKpublications.com
Charlotte, North Carolina

World map background on cover and interior by Porcupen/Shutterstock.com. Old photo backgrounds in interior by auzure 1/Shutterstock.com. Photo illustrations by SPARK Publications.

Printed in the United States of America.
First Edition softcover, July 2020, ISBN: 9781943070855
E-book, July 2020, ISBN: 9781943070893
Library of Congress Control Number: 2020904433

The author has tried to recreate events, locales, and conversations from his and his mother's memories to the best of his ability. In order to maintain anonymity in some instances, he has changed the names of some individuals and places and may have changed some identifying characteristics and details such as physical properties, occupations, and places of residence.

Praise for *A Mother's Promise*

"Bol Maywal delivers a gripping narrative of his widowed mother's treacherous journey with her young children from her war-torn village in the south of Sudan during Sudan's second civil war to difficult moments in a refugee camp and finally to the safety of the United States. His account is a moving tribute to his mother's strength, faith, fortitude, and will to survive to successfully provide a better life for her children."

– Ambassador (retired) Susan D. Page
first United States ambassador to the
Republic of South Sudan (2011-2014)

"Bol Maywal has written an extraordinary book about heroic virtue. He brilliantly paints a vivid picture of a woman, his mother, whose faith, hope, and love ultimately overcome every hardship and adversity that she encounters. Her life story will provide you with an inspiration and encouragement to overcome, and persevere through, the most difficult challenges that life can throw at you. And if that were not enough, you will be heartened to see the life of a mother through the eyes of a loving son so moved by gratitude that he felt compelled to share it with the world. I highly recommend to you *A Mother's Promise*."

– Dr. Bill Thierfelder
President of Belmont Abbey College

"*A Mother's Promise* gives fascinating insight into the adaptability of immigrants in a foreign land. It highlights not only the adversities, hardships, and traumas Bol and his family faced but also the beauty, history, and lessons of the South Sudanese culture. It shows us resilience in the face of hardship and the strength of a mother on a mission."

– Adut Bulgak
South Sudanese-Canadian professional athlete,
first South Sudanese female to play in the Women's
National Basketball Association (WNBA)

Mediterranean Sea
Sahara
AFRICA
South
Sudan
ECUATOR

**This book is dedicated to
my brave mother,
Adout Goi Ungua.**

Happy the son whose faith in his mother
remains unchanged, and who, through
all his wanderings, has kept some filial
token to repay her brave and tender love.

– Louisa May Alcott, *Little Men*

Acknowledgments

First and foremost, I would like to thank my mother, Adout Goi Ungua, for being the source of my motivation in my life. She has always been my cheerleader while being a mother and a father at the same time. Mum, your guidance and wisdom has shaped my life to be a fine young man. I thank my friend Nkiru Obi for editing several chapters of this book and Mrs. Deborah Bowen, an amazing Rotarian, for her unyielding support and for editing the rest of the chapters while I was studying at the University of Bradford in Bradford, England. Nkiru Obi and Mrs. Deborah Bowen, your incredible work has made this book possible. I also thank former United States Ambassador to the Republic of South Sudan Susan D. Page and Dr. Bill Thierfelder, president of Belmont Abbey College, for reading the book and providing endorsements for the back cover. From the bottom of my heart, I thank you very much for the encouragement and support you all have given me. I am grateful to say the least!

Table of Contents

Prologue 1

CHAPTER 1: The Chief's Favored Daughter 5

CHAPTER 2: The Healing Power of Love............................ 17

CHAPTER 3: A Journey into Egypt 29

CHAPTER 4: Hostile Refuge 37

CHAPTER 5: The Shores of Freedom 53

CHAPTER 6: Teenage Boys in America 69

CHAPTER 7: Entrepreneurial Heritage............................. 81

CHAPTER 8: Knowledge, Power & Peace.......................... 97

CHAPTER 9: A Future Leader.. 119

CHAPTER 10: Unsung Hero 129

CHAPTER 11: Family Reunion.. 141

CHAPTER 12: The Father Who Wasn't 155

CHAPTER 13: Love and Romance 165

CHAPTER 14: A Mother's Promise Fulfilled...................... 187

Children of Adout Goi Ungua... 192

Works Cited 193

About the Author... 195

UNITED STATES of AMERICA
Charlotte
North Carolina
Pacific
Ocean
Atlantic
Ocean
TROPIC OF CANCER
ECUATOR
TROPIC OF CAPRICORN

Prologue

I could call myself a city boy because I grew up in Charlotte, North Carolina, but that's only part of my story. In 2016, I traveled to the Republic of South Sudan—the native home of my mother and her people, the Luos. There, I was reunited with family members whom I heard about through my mother's stories. While I was in Panjab, I was able to experience African village life for the first time. Everything felt so surreal, and I could not believe that I was reconnected with my roots. I am the first child among my surviving siblings who made it to the United States to pay a visit to Mum's village. It was amazing!

In this Luo village, people feel the pleasure of living surrounded by everything God created, such as the animals, the trees, and the beautiful green land. This village gives them a sense of belonging and freedom to appreciate the beauty of nature and life, and it is rich with natural resources, history, and culture. The Luos are known for their warm friendship, hospitality, and peaceful coexistence with their neighbors. When outsiders visit the village, they are greeted, "Welcome to Panjab village!"

The Luo are a Nilotic people found in the region around Lake Victoria (or Nam Lolwe in Luo dialect), including western Kenya, northern Uganda, the Republic of South Sudan, Ethiopia, eastern Congo, and Tanzania. The Luo were once one of the largest ethnic groups in Africa, but due to colonialism and revolution movements, the group split into subtribes (Apai 2007:1). Historians from the African Great Lakes Region are not certain where the Luo people settled first, whether in Kenya or southern Sudan. According to the Luo folktales and old songs, it is believed the Luo originated in southern Sudan in approximately 3,000 BCE and migrated to Kenya and Uganda around 1500 AD. The language spoken by the Luo people is called Dholuo, and their primary forms of livelihood are farming, fishing, and raising cattle.

From these great people and this rich history came my mother. She played two roles in our lives. She is the father who never left us and the mother who has been there for us in the face of every challenge our family came across. At age twenty-five, I felt like my life has been determined by my mother's numerous sacrifices because she envisioned our life in America, a place that would give her children the opportunities she never had. In these pages, you will learn that it takes a strong woman to raise seven children.

During my sophomore year in college, the idea of writing a book came into my mind when I heard a quote by George Monbiot who said, "If wealth was the inevitable result of hard work and enterprise, every woman in Africa would be a millionaire." I agreed with his quote 100 percent! My mother embodies the strength and hard work of African women. The biggest gift I have had in my life is the unconditional love from my mother and guidance of my family. One thing I realized at the age of fifteen was that I cannot ignore the struggle and the sacrifice my mother made for our sakes. If I took her for granted, I could not forgive myself, nor would God forgive me.

The traditional oral storytelling of Africa is something future generations of my family may not completely understand, especially those born in the United States. This book recounts my mother's journey from a southern Sudan village to her life today in America. These stories form the basis of knowledge about our rich family history, so Mum's grandchildren will know about their brave grandmother who worked hard and sacrificed so much for us to reach the "shores of freedom" in America. Throughout this book, my goal is to share my mother's promise, wisdom, courage, struggles, and triumphs for her grandchildren, friends, and others.

I also hope this book will give hope to those who were raised by a single mother or widow and help change the minds of those who take their parents for granted. The Bible says, "Honor your father and your mother, so that you may live long in the land the Lord your God is giving you" (Exodus 20:12 NIV).

Mediterranean Sea
Sahara
AFRICA
South Sudan
ECUATOR

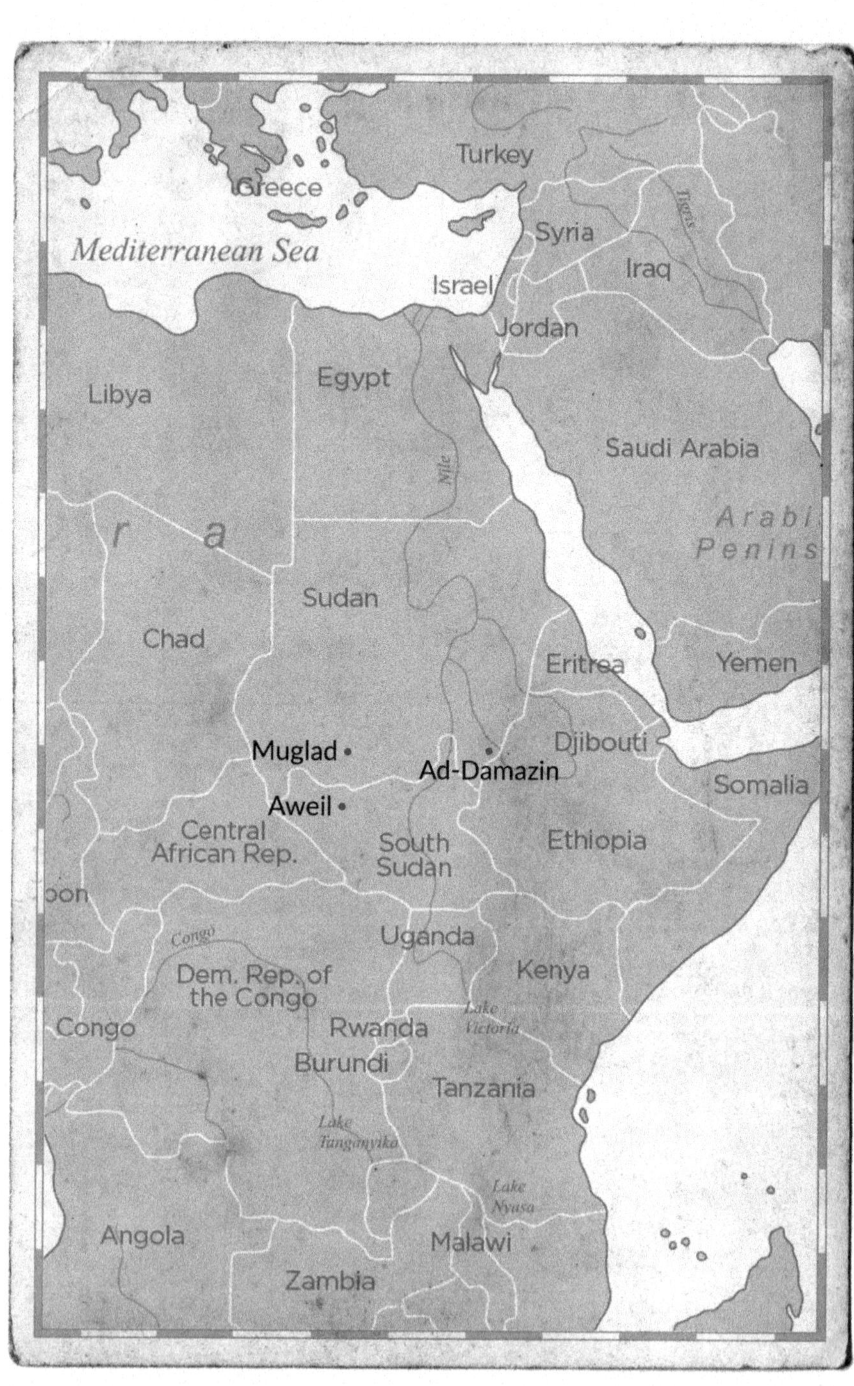

Turkey
Greece
Syria
Iraq
Mediterranean Sea
Israel
Jordan
Tigris
Libya
Egypt
Saudi Arabia
Nile
Arabi
Penins
r a
Sudan
Chad
Eritrea
Yemen
Muglad
Ad-Damazin
Djibouti
Aweil
Somalia
Central
African Rep.
South
Sudan
Ethiopia
oon
Congo
Uganda
Kenya
Dem. Rep. of
the Congo
Congo
Rwanda
Lake
Victoria
Burundi
Tanzania
Lake
Tanganyika
Lake
Nyasa
Angola
Malawi
Zambia

CHAPTER 1

The Chief's Favored Daughter

**The sun does not forget a village
just because it is small.**

– African Proverb

Adout Goi Ungua, my mother, was born in Panjab, a small village near a small city called Aweil in the Republic of South Sudan. Her actual birth date is unknown because her birthday was never recorded, not uncommon in those times. My mother claimed to be fifteen years old in 1972 when the peace agreement that ended the First Sudanese Civil War was signed between the government of Sudan and the Southern Sudan Liberation Movement. Based on this historic agreement, we believe she was born in 1957.

Goi Ungua Goi and Abuk Lual Makuach were my mother's parents. Grandma was born in the heart of Dinka land in Gorgrial, Warrap, which lies east of the Northern Bahr el Ghaza region. She came from the Dinka ethnic group, which is the largest in South Sudan. Grandpa came from the Luo ethnic group, which is among the smallest. Both my parents were from families of ten children, and my mother is the third oldest child (from her mother and father). Ethnically, Mum is a mix of Luo and Dinka but identifies as Luo.

In Luo culture, the father determines a child's ethnic identity. My siblings and I are Luos, but Dinka blood runs through our veins from our grandmother's side.

Grandpa was a polygamist. He had seven wives and fathered twenty-one children. Four of his wives were Dinkas, and the other three were Luos. Unfortunately, some of his wives left him because they could not get along with the others. My grandpa founded Panjab village in the early 1900s by clearing the land and chasing away the animals. His family was first to settle there. Originally, the newly founded land was called Amou-Guak, which means "peanuts" in Dinka dialect, due to its abundance of peanuts. Shortly after he discovered the new land, he was unanimously chosen to lead his people and served as chief of Panjab village for decades. He was admired by many people including the Dinka ethnic group who lived side by side with the Luos.

As a chief, Grandpa governed his people peacefully under a huge tree called Quel. This tree was basically his "office" where he led his people and solved disputes between different ethnic groups or individuals in the community. His role was not limited to conflict resolution. He had executive, legislative, and spiritual roles as chief. Grandpa saw Christianity and Islam as foreign religions. Therefore, he faithfully practiced animism, a purely indigenous belief system that predates all organized religions and was the spiritual practice of most ancient cultures all over the world. Animists believe that all people, plants, objects, and natural phenomena have a spirit that animates them, and all these spirits are connected. They also believe in ancestral spirits and their powers to influence events and communicate with the living.

You might classify my mother's family as middle class. Though Grandpa was a chief and very well respected, he had little material wealth. Instead, he had a large farm five miles outside Panjab in a place called Machar where he grew crops such as peanuts and sorghum and raised cows, goats, chickens, and sheep for the family's needs and to trade. He was also an ironsmith and made hoes, spears, and arrows to trade with his neighbors. And he was a beekeeper, fisherman, and hunter.

Grandma was also a farmer and had her own farm in Panjab. Her farm was small, but she contributed to maintain food security. Under Grandpa's leadership, his family and the villagers in Panjab were self-sufficient.

Mum once told me that she considered herself very lucky because she was not forced into an early, arranged marriage. In Panjab village, girls as young as thirteen were married off by their parents in exchange for a dowry, usually in the form of cattle. The Luos are one of the wealthiest cattle-owning societies in Africa. Cattle are a symbol of wealth and source of pride. Most of the village girls were not happy because their interest was not a factor in their marriage process. Mum hoped to choose a man of her own free will, and she liked a young man who was interested in her. The mutual interest between them seemed promising and could serve as a path out of an arranged marriage in the Luo culture. But the fact that Mum was a daughter of a respected chief in her village did not make things easy for her. Men from different ethnic groups came to the old man asking how many cows Grandpa would take for his favored daughter.

The young man Mum liked went to Khartoum to get his education and promised to return. One day, several men who were serious about wanting to marry Mum came and spoke to the old man. The first promised to pay a dowry of sixty to seventy-five cattle, with more to follow. The second raised his dowry payment to ninety cattle plus more once the deal was sealed. The old man was annoyed by young men who kept coming to talk to him about his daughter, so he spoke to Mum about several people who showed interest in her.

"A girl should not be married before she reaches the age of twenty," she told him with a voice of polite dissent. Grandpa and Mum enjoyed a good father-daughter relationship, but grandpa neither agreed nor disagreed with what his daughter had to say. She tried to convince him to hold off on her marriage, saying she was not ready, to buy more time for the young man in Khartoum to complete his studies and return to the village. I asked Mum what made that young man so special from everyone else. She said he was a gentleman and educated, very nice and respectful. The qualities she saw in him are no different from what any intelligent woman wants in a man today. His desire for an education showed his ambition. Mum cherished education and wanted it for herself, but she was denied that right by a society that did not allow girls to go to school.

At age fifteen, my mother still did not welcome the idea of marriage. Since there was mutual interest between her and the young man in Khartoum, there was no rush from either side, and it seemed like a win-win situation for my mother, her family, and the young man. This was her plan at least. But Mum was born into a society where wealth was measured by how many cows and how much land the family had. So people married their daughters off for economic reasons or to buy allegiance from families that had wealth and political status. Chief's daughters were not off the hook from the way the society did things. Mum was still hoping that things would work out as she planned, but the clock was slowly turning against her as more men continued to ask for her hand in marriage.

In Africa, rites of passage play a central role in socialization, demarking the different stages in an individual's development as well as that person's relationship and role to the broader community. Young women like my mother had to undergo rites of passage in order to be considered woman. Three key marks of distinction are found across the Luo ethnic groups: scarification, tattooing, and body piercing. In Luo culture, these marks are distinctive aspects of culture and rites of passage and form the identity of groups. In all cases, they double as a form of body adornment.

Scarification is the practice of piercing the skin with a sharp object in a controlled way on various parts of the body in order to create marks of distinction. Scarification (in African culture as a whole) communicates gender, age, social status, and more to the community who knows what these powerful signs mean. Traditional scarification is believed to have healing powers, enhance beauty, and is an important part of ethnic identity and rites of passages to mark stages in the life process, such as puberty and marriage. The piercing can be done with glass, knives, stones, or even a coconut shell. It is common to apply caustic plant juices, ground charcoal, ash, or gun powder after the piercing is complete in order to provide the desired emphasis. It's a painful process but one all young people must go through. Mum has traditional marks on her cheeks and body that were made by skilled practitioners. The cheek marks identify her as belonging to the Luo ethnic group.

In Luo culture, the scarifications on a woman's body demonstrate the woman's bravery. Scarification is an outward sign that a woman exhibits her willingness to bear pain. A woman with scars is asserting that she is strong enough to endure the extreme pain of childbirth. Traditionally, marking for boys and girls takes place between the ages of twelve and thirteen, although girls receive an additional series of vertical cuts on their backs. This is done to symbolize gender lines and differentiate them from boys. After having these scars done, the girl is then considered an adult and is deemed ready for marriage. At age thirteen, Mum received her scars on both sides of her cheeks along with other traditional tattoos.

Arranged marriage eventually caught up with her at age sixteen. In 1972, a tall, dark-skinned Luo man approached my grandfather, the chief, for my mother. The man was probably in his late twenties, if not in his early thirties. He was a respected warrior in the village and wore his long hair in braids. The Dinka community knew him by the name Bol Ma-nyang, and his Luo tribesmen called him by his Luo traditional name, Uchu Maywal. He decorated himself with beaded jewelry that made him unique and powerful in the eyes of many. And he carried his spear with the pride of a warrior. He would forever change the life of a young village girl.

Once again, the old man came and spoke with his daughter about a man who wanted her. Mum was not afraid to speak her mind and told her father she was not interested in Uchu. Grandpa returned to Uchu Maywal and apologized, saying my mother was not interested, but Grandpa promised to continue talking to Mum on Uchu's behalf. Uchu came a second time. The old man again apologized to Uchu and said he couldn't change the girl's mind. This fell onto Uchu's deaf ears. Uchu came a third time with a dowry of 100 cows and brought his people along. Mum still refused, but the people who influenced the final decision were her uncles, relatives, and elders in the family. My grandparents finally supported the idea, and Mum was betrothed. My mother was not happy, and her parents feared she might run away. So Grandpa ordered guards to follow her until the marriage ceremony was complete.

At the end of 1972, my mother was forced to marry Uchu Maywal against her will. Cows were slaughtered at the celebration, and the traditional Luo dances were performed. Relatives and close family friends came to cook all different types of South Sudanese dishes, and other young women went to collect water for the big day. At the traditional wedding ceremony, a lot of the people came from different parts of Aweil to witness the wedding. People danced, laughed, ate, and celebrated. Mum was still unhappy, but she respected her parents and the traditions of her people. Her own happiness was overshadowed by the interest of elders, relatives, and males who would benefit from her marriage.

The school boy returned later to find that Mum would not be his, but he didn't give up, even after she was married. Whenever Mum went to collect water from the river, he would be there waiting for her, attempting to win her back. He once told her that he would risk his life by running away with her. But Mums's obedience to her parents, tradition, and husband was bigger than the love the young man had for her. He eventually accepted the reality that it was too late for him and Mum, so he gave up and went back to Khartoum where he completed his education and became a federal wildlife officer.

The first year of mother's marriage was a challenge as she learned to be a wife in her new home. Everything happened so fast, and she had to learn to adapt. At age seventeen, she gave birth to her first child. By age nineteen, she had three children, all girls.

In Sudanese culture, boys and girls may be favored by different groups for different reasons. Having girls is considered a good thing because the girls will be married off and bring in dowries. Boys, on the other hand, grow up to become men who carry their families' names; they perform the last rites at their parents' funerals and play other important roles that shape the society.

My paternal grandmother, Grandma Akol, was definitely on the side with a pervasive preference for boys. When my mother gave birth to her fourth daughter, Grandma Akol went to her son and complained about him marrying a woman who only brought girls. She went so far as to suggest that he take my mother back to her parents and have some of his dowry returned.

Imagine being a young woman at age nineteen, married to a man who never won your heart in the first place, and having to deal with an old woman who demands something that you have no control over. Of course, Uchu did not see any reason to return his wife and asked his mother to be patient. He told Grandma Akol that a child's gender was determined not by a woman but by God. Grandma apologized to her son's wife, and Mum accepted the apology.

In September 1983, the region around Aweil, including Panjab, came under attack by government forces in the beginning of the Second Sudanese Civil War. My mother's village was burned to ashes by aircrafts. The systematic and brutal nature of the destruction and the attacks on civilians using military aircraft were intended to displace the population from their villages. The government in Khartoum wanted to control the Northern Bhar el Ghazel region. Government forces killed children, elders, and women. They swept across the land looting properties that belonged to innocent people, destroying food stocks, and raping young girls and women. All men and teenage boys who resisted were shot at point-blank range in front of their families. My mother saw her husband shot and killed that day. Thousands of people ran to the bush to hide and save their lives.

At her mother's encouragement, my mother gathered up her surviving children—my sister Aketch and brother Allah-jabo (her first son, a toddler whom she tied to her back)—and fled into the bush with others from her village. She left behind three daughters who had died young of natural causes and were buried in the village and her parents, sisters, and brothers, knowing she might never see them again. At age twenty-six, my mother became a widow and was left to raise her children on her own while leaving the only home she had ever known. She prayed for the Almighty God to guide them safely out of that place where bullets came down like rain and heavy smoke covered everything.

My mother and her fellow villagers embarked on a more than 500-mile journey toward a displacement camp in northern Sudan. Arab soldiers from northern Sudan were closing in on the marshland in the remote area around Aweil. The soldiers fired indiscriminately at the fleeing villagers, but Mum's group managed to stay low and quiet and dodge bullets that flew over their heads as they maneuvered through thick, swampy land.

An infant cried and revealed the hideout of a second group behind my mother. Soldiers traced the noise and shot and killed everyone in that group, including the baby. Other groups learned from this incident as they tried to avoid Arab soldiers from detecting their movement in the bush. Newborns and young children were considered security threats for many who feared for their lives and hoped to make it out of the war zone without being killed. To ensure survival of the maximum number of lives possible and for the greater good of the group, mothers sacrificed their children who could not be kept silent, especially when the enemy was nearby. Some women silently killed their young, suffocating them with their bare hands, and others killed their children by breaking their necks. Children who were noisy or who constantly cried asking for food and water were the main targets. Babies and children who were too weak to make it were finished off by their mothers.

These circumstances put pressure on mothers with young children. But there was no way my mother would be complicit in that kind of policy. She had already lost many friends, her husband, and relatives when her village was attacked, and she could not afford to lose any of her children. In a worst-case scenario, my mother would have preferred to give her own life to see her children and others survive. Mum believed that children must not be killed even if by doing so they could save more lives. She and other women in the group stood shoulder to shoulder and agreed that it was wrong to kill the innocents and were prepared to prohibit it regardless of the circumstances.

For weeks, my mother and many others fought for survival on their journey northward as they walked mile after mile. During the day, they hid and rested and traveled mostly during the night. They survived by eating peanuts, fish, and wild fruits. They slept on the ground and in areas that provided good cover and concealment, fighting off mosquitoes and other insects all the while. People dropped dead of starvation when there was nothing to eat. My mother had enough dry peanuts for her children when she could not find other food. They went days without food and dug holes in the ground for water to drink. The World Food Program only dropped food in areas where there was no conflict taking place between the rebels and Arab government forces. Under the cover of darkness and at the mercy of wild animals that could attack them, my mother and her group continued to march on with the hope that they would reach a safe location sooner rather than later. They avoided using the main roads and kept silent during their movement.

They settled first in a displacement camp in Muglad, a city in northern Sudan about 150 miles northeast of Aweil, although they walked much farther on their indirect route. Muglad was consistently screened by northern Sudanese army forces and General Intelligence Service to make sure there weren't rebels among the displaced people. When the city came under attack, my mother and others set out again for a safer place.

After more weeks of travel on foot, they arrived at Ad-Damazin in northern Sudan, the capital of the Blue Nile State. They sought refuge at a displacement camp where they did not hear guns fired at them anymore and where the United Nations Mission in Sudan (UNMIS) provided assistance. The area was calm and peaceful.

Thank God, my mother and siblings made it out of the war zone. They escaped the bloody and protracted civil war that cost the lives of 2.5 million people and forced thousands upon thousands to become displaced refugees. It is an understatement to say that war, and this war in particular, was filled with hard times, loss of life, and suffering.

"Quel" is a huge tree where my mother's father, Chief Goi Ungua, sat and governed his community peacefully for decades. Quel is believed to be over 100 years old.

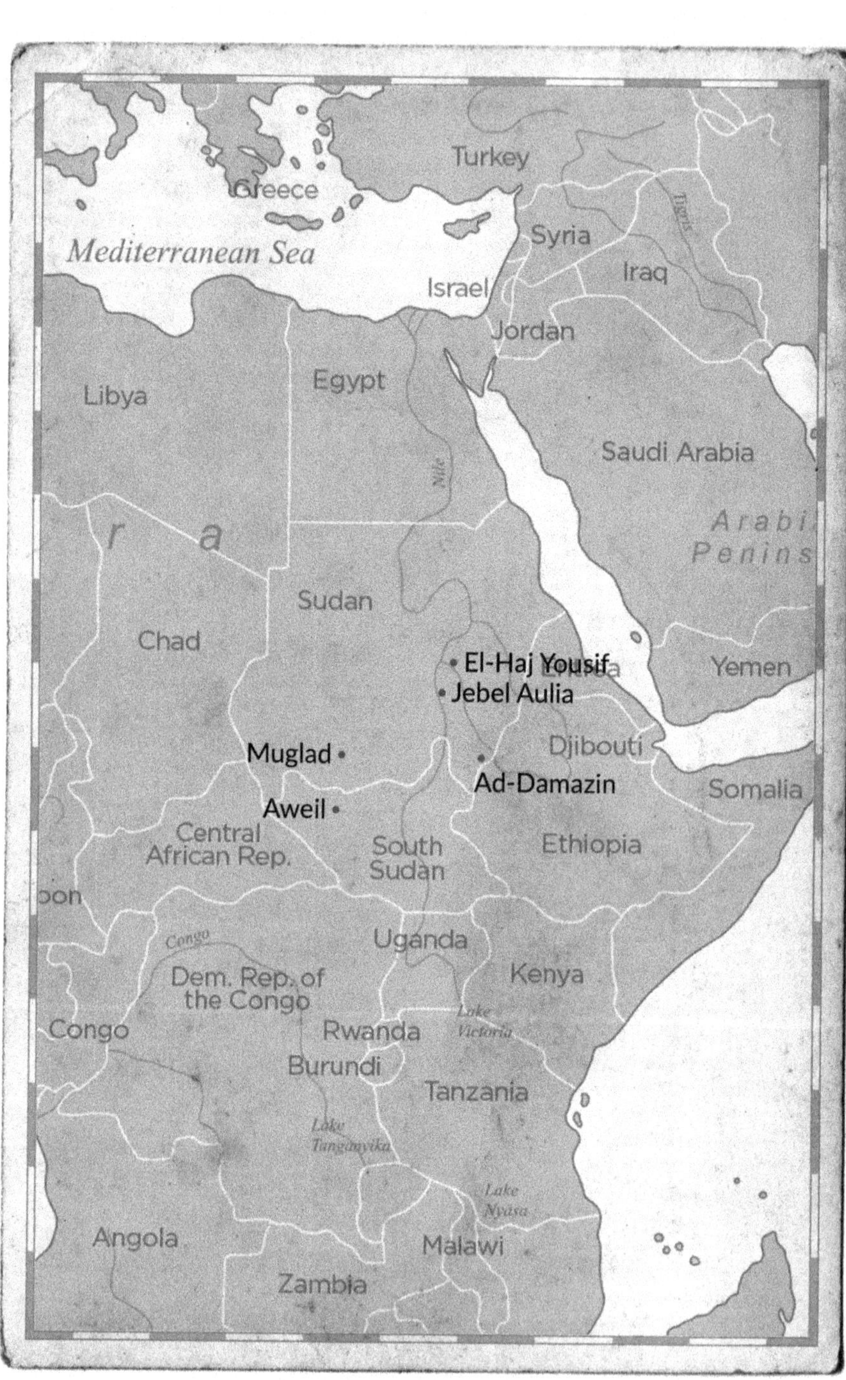

Greece
Turkey
Mediterranean Sea
Syria
Israel
Iraq
Tigris
Jordan
Libya
Egypt
Saudi Arabia
Arabi
Penins
Nile
Sudan
Chad
El-Haj Yousif
Jebel Aulia
Yemen
Muglad
Djibouti
Ad-Damazin
Somalia
Aweil
Central
African Rep.
South
Sudan
Ethiopia
Congo
Uganda
Dem. Rep. of
the Congo
Kenya
Congo
Rwanda
Lake
Victoria
Burundi
Tanzania
Lake
Tanganyika
Lake
Nyasa
Angola
Malawi
Zambia

CHAPTER 2

The Healing Power of Love

Through the praise of children and infants you have established a stronghold against your enemies, to silence the foe and the avenger.

– Psalm 8:2 (NIV)

I took my first breath in a world where death among infants was an everyday occurrence. It was also a difficult time in Sudan when the country was experiencing a famine followed by the heaviest rainy season ever recorded in Sudan's history. I was born on November 27, 1989, in the District Nine (aka "block 9") displacement camp in the El-Haj Yousif district near Khartoum, Sudan. El-Haj Yousif was populated by thousands of displaced people who fled the war zone in southern Sudan.

After my Mum and siblings arrived in the displacement camp, other extended family members came as well, including Uchu Maywal's family members who would father my siblings Amal, Maywal, Amoe, and Makot, and me. As is tradition in Sudanese culture, all of Mum's children carry the Maywal name and are legally considered Uchu Maywal's children because he paid the dowry for her when she was a young girl.

It wasn't until I was fifteen that I learned the details of my birth. Mum said I cried a lot because I was not happy. Why wouldn't I cry? I was born in a country that knew war since its independence from Britain and Egypt in the 1950s. It was a cruel and nasty world where Arabs were free and Africans were slaves. Displaced people, including my family, were forced to starve in their own country and lived in hardship in camps where sickness struck. The human rights of Africans are constantly violated by Islamic fundamentalists who wish to create an Islamic and Arab state in an African country. All these were compelling reasons that would cause anybody to cry, including a newborn child when he first enters this cold world.

In southern Sudan, the rebels continued to fight bravely against the oppressive regime in order to free the indigenous people from Arab domination and oppression. Every day was a struggle in the displacement camp. The mortality rate for children was substantially above the emergency threshold. Many were at risk of dying before they reached age five.

Just three weeks from my fourth birthday, I became seriously ill. I was wrapped in a dirty piece of blanket to keep me warm as I awaited death to release me from suffering. My biological father, Akol Dagan, wished death upon me because the agony that I endured was too much for him. Relatives and family friends expected me to die within three days, but my mother refused to see me go. She fought for my life with faith instead of medicine, rebelling against everybody's expectations and the fate that took many children's lives.

I survived the first week, and signs of recovery began to appear slowly. By the third week, I gained enough strength to walk on my own for the first time since becoming ill. My siblings saw that remarkable moment and erupted in celebration, clapping their hands for the miracle that I was able to see my fourth birthday.

My mother once shared an interesting yet somehow frightening story. When she was nine months pregnant with me, something terrible happened to her. Life in displacement camps was unpredictable, and at times the UN aid would not come through in the camp where we lived. As a result, Mum turned to brewing and selling alcohol to feed the family. In the alcohol business, nothing brought customers more than a winning personality and a kind heart, which my mother had in abundance. She was known for her work ethic, determination, and kindness by customers and her friends. Mum was a very likeable person, but one woman did not like her. This woman, Akout, wanted Mum dead, along with the innocent child in her womb, to put her out of business because they were competitors. Akout was so jealous of my mother's success that she resorted to witchcraft.

Mum was returning home after leaving a house where a group of women brewed alcohol together. Akout followed Mum for a while without Mum's knowledge. Suddenly, Akout came behind her and performed black magic that caused Mum to fall forward, as if someone had pushed her. My mother described feeling a heavy wind-like force that thrust her from behind and threw her to the ground. There she lay on her stomach, unconscious for a long period of time, alone.

Luckily, one of Mum's good friends was heading home from visiting a relative and saw my mother's body lying there lifeless. When she got close to the body, she exclaimed, "Oh, God! It's a pregnant woman!" Then she rolled the body over and immediately discovered it was my mother. "Adout, open your eyes," she said. "What happened?" Mum did not respond, so her friend began to scream for help. My Mum's friend put her head against Mum's chest to check for breathing and a heartbeat, and to her relief, she heard a slow, rhythmic heartbeat. Water was brought to wash Mum's face, and some was poured on her head in attempt to revive her. When their attempt to revive her failed, they picked her up and carried her back to the displacement camp.

Is the baby okay in the womb? That was the question running through the minds of family and neighbors who had heard what happened. It was no easy night for Mum as she struggled with pain. Nobody knew exactly what had happened to her. The whole night was consumed with prayers, tears, and hopes that she would recover quickly.

By noon the next day, Mum started to open her eyes and had no idea what happened. Her entire body was in so much pain. She could barely move her fingers or even lift her arms or legs on her own. She lay on the bed as family and friends gathered around her to comfort her as much as possible since there was no hospital nearby for her to go to. One of her friends suggested that Mum be taken to see an elderly lady who was believed to be a woman of God. The lady had a reputation for helping others and would be more than happy to help.

Upon arrival at the old lady's house, the woman saw the agony Mum was in and said, "Let me do a prayer before we begin." My Mum, sister, and her friend agreed. As she was praying for my mother, God's presence and glory filled the room, and miracles were taking place. After her prayer, Mum felt better, and then the elderly woman revealed to my mother what really happened.

She told Mum about Akout and her attempt to kill Mum and the baby through black magic. Mum was astonished and speechless when she heard all this! After the woman explained everything step by step, she did something that was quite remarkable. She said she could see me inside my mother's womb. The elderly woman was believed to have a supernatural ability that enabled her eyes to see clearly through my mother's womb, with more clarity than an ultrasound used in today's advanced technology. "I see him; it's a boy!" the woman said with a smile on her face. She was even able to detect my heart beat and body parts.

"The baby got scared when you were pushed by the force. He is tired, and you're tired as well. Don't worry, everything will be fine," she told Mum. "Your due date was the same day Akout planned her evil work. Did you know that?"

"No, I did not," said Mum.

"Currently, the baby is not in the right position. I'll put the baby in the right position, and then you can go home. Your body needs rest before you can deliver," she explained. "You will deliver just fine. God bless you," she declared.

"Thank you for everything, and God will return the favor," was Mum's response.

Through her supernatural ability, the elderly woman was able to tell Mum in detail about the health, position, and gender of her baby, the past and future due date, and the jealously that led to all this trouble in detail. Something that ordinarily would be humanly impossible was done by this awesome older woman to save my life. Never mind the harsh conditions that awaited me out in the world and the continued struggle Mum had to go through after my birth. Despite all that, we survived the work of an evil woman.

My siblings were there to witness my birth and welcome me to the world the next day at 1:00 p.m. I was given the name Uchu, the traditional Luo name of my traditional father who paid the dowry to marry my mother. It was an honor to be given his name! Although I am not the biological son of Uchu Maywal, he was still my father regardless of my biological father's identity.

When I was fifteen years old, my mother shared this story with me. This is what my Mum told me about the day she met me after all the pain she went through. "When I had you, Uchu, the first thing I remember is that you were a handsome baby. I saw that you had super-white eyes, beautiful skin, thick eyebrows, and jet-black hair. By far, your skin tone was the lightest compared to your siblings. Then I opened the blanket you were wrapped up in to make sure you were not hurt. I had fallen badly days before I had you. I was in so much pain and was worried more about you than my own self when I regained consciousness. I took off the blanket to make sure you did not have any broken bones. I checked your head, back, fingers, and your little toes. Once I was reassured that you were okay, I was able to breathe a sigh of relief and thank the Almighty God that you were healthy. I was overcome with joy as I held you in my arms that very first day. I knew I would never let any harm come into my children's lives."

Out of curiosity, I asked my mother what had happened to the evil lady, Akout. "She disappeared and relocated to a different camp with the thought that she had succeeded in killing us," she told me.

In this world, people of God exist and are empowered by Him to do extraordinary things. The elderly woman who helped my mother was gifted. Her presence in the displacement camp was a huge help to those who needed it. The Bible tells us that faith without works is dead (James 2:17). The power of anointing is given to help other people in a supernatural way, and in the process, it reveals God's mighty power over evil. The elderly woman laid her hand on my mother's belly while she prayed and asked God to stir up and manifest the gifts of the Holy Spirit that are within all of us. As she asked God to stir them up, He did! Mum felt better after seeing her, and I was born healthy.

There is evil in this world, and there is good also. The truth is there are people who are spirituality gifted to help others through the mighty work of God. Spiritual gifts of healing, working miracles, teaching, and faith are all invaluable manifestations for those chosen by God. Had Mum not seen the elderly woman that fateful day, the story of my life and hers would have been something else entirely. I am a living testimony that God is always good, even when humans are not.

In 1994, the Islamic regime in Sudan decided to relocate all the displaced persons who resided in El-Haj Yousif where I was born. The government brought in troops and loaded thousands of us on lorry trucks and dumped us miles away in an open field in Jebel Aulia. Aketch was fortunate in that she had already married and was not further displaced with the rest of us. The new site was a flat ground with no access to clean water, food, or a hospital. My parents built us a small tent using trees branches.

My stepfather, James Nagan (who came into our lives shortly after my fourth birthday), left to search for a job while the family stayed behind. A week after he was gone, conditions became even worse when the camp flooded after a heavy rain. Many people were forced to sleep standing with their children in their arms. Many others drowned because they could not swim.

Mum was alone with nobody to assist her as the water level continued to rise. The frame for our makeshift tent was a thick piece of wood held up by two tree branches at each end. Mum put Amal, Maywal, and me on the roof of the tent and asked us to stay there while she took Amoe, the youngest at the time, to safety. She asked us to conquer fear and not move or else we were all going to drown. We sat a few inches above the water and held on tight despite our terror. Mum tied beans, oil, groundnuts, and maize on her back and put Amoe on her shoulders as she walked through the water to find higher ground. Allah-jabo was old enough to keep his head above the water as he followed Mum to safety. Once she reached higher ground that was safe enough, Mum left Amoe with Allah-jabo and returned to grab the next youngest child (me) and took me to safety. Again, she returned to grab Maywal and other things while Amal hung on. Before our tent completely collapsed, Mum returned just in time to rescue Amal. This time Mum walked on her toes as the water reached her neck.

From the start, the living conditions in the Jebel Aulia camp were life-threating due to overcrowding and lack of water and sanitation. Thousands of people jammed together allowed disease to pass easily from one person to another. Among the diseases running rampant were cholera, malaria, tuberculosis, diarrhea, blood dysentery, mental illness, anemia, and many different skin diseases. Malaria was the most grievous and killed numerous camp residents on a daily basis. It was so widespread because the camp was located close to a river where tall, thick grasses were an ideal breeding ground for thousands of mosquitoes. They also bred in stagnant pools surrounding the camp. The mosquito attacks were virtually unavoidable because we had no mosquito nets or mosquito repellent. When they bit us, they spread a poison into our bodies that often resulted in death.

My siblings and I suffered from malaria as children from time to time. I remember vividly the day I was struck by malaria as a little boy.

I remember feeling constant pain all over my body. The pain was so severe and got worse each day followed by a systemic headache, a dry cough, nausea, and vomiting. Malaria typically produces a string of recurrent attacks, or paroxysms, each of which has three stages—chills, then fever, then sweating. I was so sick that I was near death and could not eat for days. I lost significant weight as my body became weaker each day that I continued to battle malaria. A hospital would have been able to help, but there was no hospital for us.

Throughout all our struggles, our mother showed us her unconditional love. She held all of us warmly in her arms, not only when we were born but also when we were ill and near death. When illness struck her children, my mother battled alongside us. My brother Maywal was diagnosed with chicken pox and malnutrition at the same time. My mother never gave up on him; instead, she sacrificed her sleep and fought alongside him to get rid of this contagious illness. A year after I was born, I suffered from acute malnutrition, the number one killer among children under five years old in the displacement camp. This illness was so severe that I could not walk for two years. She was there for me day and night to nourish and care for me. At one time, my brother Amoe became ill and was knocking on death's door. My mother tried traditional medication and even took him to the hospital with the little savings she had. Later, my brother Makot was very ill, and his condition was uncertain. My mother sold all her possessions to purchase medicine to give him life.

My siblings and I were all born during the Second Sudanese Civil War. There was no birth center or hospital for my Mum to give birth. There was no epidural to ease the birthing pains, so Mum had to give birth to all of us naturally in the worst conditions imaginable. There was no running water, no electricity, nor adequate food to feed us. My mother shouldered most of the responsibilities for our family and its survival on her own. Life was a struggle for her, but my mother's bravery and her unconditional love stood the test of time.

The difficult experiences that my mother went through over and over serve as evidence that a mother's love for her children is powerful. That's what I call unconditional love.

Mum always put us before herself. While living in the displacement camps, she made sure that we attended school. Using the little savings she had, she registered my older brother Allah-jabo and my sister Amal to attend Comboni Missionary School in Al-Shijra near Khartoum. She refused to allow any circumstance to stop her children from receiving an education. She made sure my siblings had uniforms for school along with writing utensils. She woke up at 6 a.m. to walk them to school because she knew that education was power. When she cooked for the family, she was the last one to eat and drink water. Her utmost priority was making sure our bellies were full, even if that meant she had to go hungry. She made sure we had clean water to quench our thirst, even if that meant she had to walk seven miles to fetch water.

My mother is a strong and remarkable African woman. She is an angel whose love continues to guide my family. All that I am and all that I'll ever be would not be possible if Mum had not poured her blessings and love on me. I love her and owe her a limitless debt! She is the most caring, patient, determined, resilient, and hard-working woman I know. She did everything for the sake of our future. My mother, Adout Goi, has never fallen short of being a mother, and to me and my siblings she always leads by example.

My mother has an unyielding faith in God. During her fifteen years in the displacement camp, she and all of her children became Christians. We had different priests who came to preach to us where we sat in groups to hear the teachings. Mum taught us to never doubt the power of prayer. She said, "If you call God with all your heart, mind, and soul, He/She will answer because God is not deaf." She was our first teacher and taught through stories about life. She is like a mother bear that sacrificed so much to take care of her baby cubs. My mother has been widowed twice in her life. Life was tough for her in the displacement camps in Sudan. Despite the difficulties, she has always endured in the face of challenges that life throws at her. With every passing day, I am constantly reminded that my mother remains an important gift to our family. She is simply the backbone of our family from the beginning until today. The impoverished living conditions in the displacement camps was a reality that demonstrated who was with us and who was not, who truly loved us and who did not. My stepfather, James Nagan, was in and out of our lives back in Sudan, but I do credit him for the times he was in.

Most of my uncles from my father's side dodged us, believing that my mother was "inferior" because she was uneducated and poor; the few who felt ashamed came to extend their greetings sometimes. My mother never asked them for anything. When we made it to United States in 2001, the same uncles who never bothered to check on us started to claim that they knew us. They would phone constantly asking for financial assistance from us now that we were in America. In South Sudanese culture, family are supposed to stick together regardless of the circumstance because blood is thicker than water. But that was not the case with some of our uncles.

My mother is a strong woman. She is a mother of ten children. She brought five boys and five girls into this world. She lost three beautiful daughters to illness in southern Sudan before she fled the civil war. She is the daughter of a village chief. She is a great role model to all her siblings. She helped raised her nephews and put them in school. She is naturally intelligent and able to speak Luo and Dinka dialects fluently. Despite the lack of a formal education, she learned to speak Sudanese Arabic. My mother gave us love and gratitude. She believes in the ability of all her children and their dreams. She nurtured and fought for all of us, not for us to give back anything, but to see us grow strong and make her proud. My mother's love is indeed instinctual, unconditional, and forever.

James Nagan poses at a family residence in the Al-Shijra displacement camp, the second camp the family lived in before being forcibly relocated to Jebel Aulia. Maywal stands behind. *Photo courtesy of Allah-jabo Maywal.*

The family lived in the house with the double door in Jebel Aulia. The South Sudanese returned to South Sudan when it gained independence on July 9, 2011. As of 2018, a displaced Nubian family who fled the war in the Nubia Mountains had moved in. *Photo courtesy of Uguak Majok.*

From left to right: Maywal Maywal, Bol Maywal, and Allah-jabo Maywal inside the family residence at Al-Shijra circa 1994. *Photo courtesy of Aketch Maywal .*

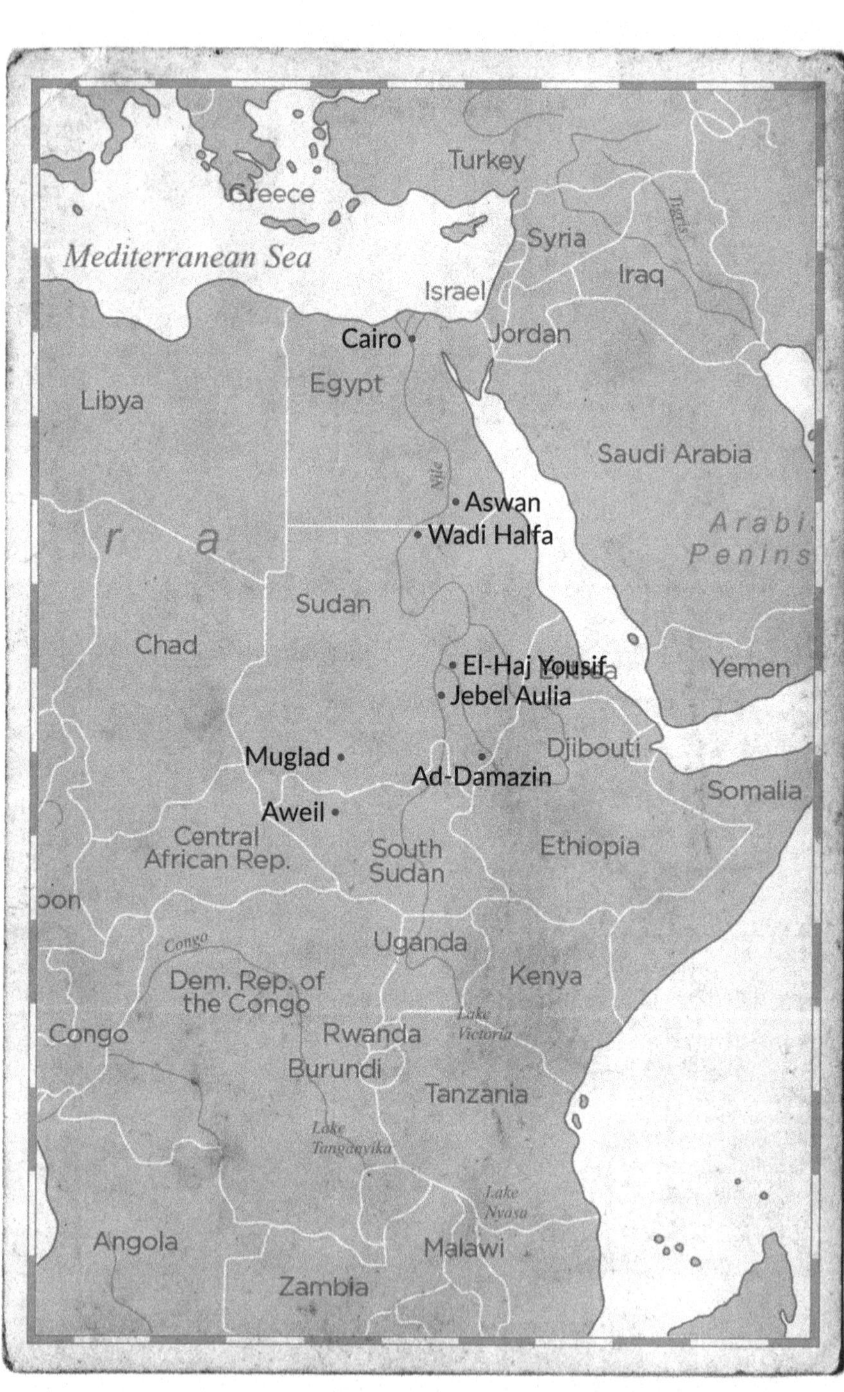

Turkey
Greece
Mediterranean Sea
Syria
Iraq
Israel
Jordan
Cairo
Egypt
Libya
Saudi Arabia
Arabi
Penins
Nile
Aswan
Wadi Halfa
Sudan
Chad
El-Haj Yousif
Yemen
Jebel Aulia
Muglad
Djibouti
Ad-Damazin
Somalia
Aweil
Central
African Rep.
South
Sudan
Ethiopia
oon
Congo
Uganda
Dem. Rep. of
the Congo
Kenya
Congo
Rwanda
Lake
Victoria
Burundi
Tanzania
Lake
Tanganyika
Lake
Nyasa
Angola
Malawi
Zambia

CHAPTER 3

A Journey into Egypt

"For I know the plans I have for you,"
declares the Lord, "plans to prosper
you and not to harm you, plans
to give you hope and a future."

– Jeremiah 29:11 (NIV)

In 1997, my family made the decision to leave Sudan due to civil war and oppression of the native black population by the Islamic regime. One night when everyone was sleeping, my mother, stepfather, Amoe, Makot, and I left Jebel Aulia. Our improbable journey of a thousand miles started with a single step into the darkness of night.

For safety reasons, my mother and stepfather told no one of our plan to escape our native country. Only my sister Aketch knew the specifics of our departure. By this time, Aketch was married and had children of her own. Allah-jabo, who was the toddler Mum carried on her back when she fled her village, and our siblings, Amal and Maywal, would initially stay behind under Aketch's care. None of us knew how profoundly leaving Sudan would change the course of our lives.

As I remember, all of us wore unmatched flip-fops that night as we stepped out on foot to start our journey into an uncertain future. My mother had a bag of roasted peanuts for us to eat along the way and carried a single gallon of water for us to drink. In her purse, she had a small silver metal cup to use for water. My stepfather carried an old bag in his hand and had approximately £100 Sudanese in cash. That was all we took as we left everyone we knew and everything we had behind us. It was very emotional to see tears drop from the eyes of Aketch and her husband, whom we might never see again.

We started out walking on foot through the darkness to a bus station where we snuck onto a bus to Khartoum. An hour later, we arrived in Khartoum, the capital of Sudan. We managed to avoid Sudan's security apparatus that night. We ended up staying with one of my mother's cousins, Aunty Awen, for a night in a smaller displacement camp outside the capital. There we ate as much as we could and rested overnight before we began the next leg of our journey the following day. In the morning, we went to Bahri train station in Khartoum to continue our journey. Bahri train station was crowded with people who were leaving Sudan for one reason or another; some were traders, and displaced people like us mixed among them.

Our train was old and agonizingly slow, but it would take us out of Sudan. The railway was the last relic of what had been the best railway network in Africa at the time of the country's independence from British rule in January 1956. Our train had first-class sleepers, first and second-class seats in compartments, and third-class open bench seats. Of course, my family was in the crowded third class with uncomfortable, hard seats and no air conditioning or seat belts for passengers. We were all miserable, but we were determined to leave Sudan behind us for a better life somewhere beyond our border. The train chugged through the mighty Nubian Desert headed for Wadi Halfa.

As we went through the countryside, we saw abandoned communities and wondered who had once lived in these areas and where they had gone. Something must have had happened that wiped them out. After three and a half days on the train with little to eat, we arrived at Wadi Halfa around 6:00 p.m. The new place did not look familiar, but it smelled fresh. We were all relieved to arrive without incident and to breathe in some of that clean, fresh air and hope for better days ahead of us.

Wadi Halfa looked nothing like the displacement camps we left behind us, so I asked my stepfather a quick question: "Will this place be our new camp?" He told me, "No, we are not there yet." When I asked him how much farther we had to go, he reminded me that we were still in Sudan. I asked him why everything was covered by sand, hills, and big, mud-brick structures. He explained that Sudan was Africa's biggest country and that we were just in a different part of Sudan. When he saw how confused I still was, he had a laugh.

My stepfather looked at me and said, "You will learn more about this beautiful country that is being destroyed by Arab domination when you go to school one day."

"Why do I have to wait that long to learn about the country?" I asked.

"It's not you having to wait that is the problem," he said. "The fact that different parts of Sudan have problems is what you will learn someday. South Sudan is a battle field. It's too complicated for me to explain to you. East Sudan has its problem. Western Sudan, Darfur region has a problem. If I tell you the politics of the civil war, you may not be able to grasp everything. You already know how brutal the Arabs treated us and the conditions we were put under. They view us as animals. We are no longer the natives of this land, nor are we second class or third class. We are slaves in their view."

His voice dropped, and I stopped asking questions. I was trying to make sense of the new place. There was no way I was going to comprehend the complicated politics of Africa's biggest country at age nine.

My family and I were exhausted and hungry from the long journey. It was so long I felt like we were in a different country. We got off the train, and my stepfather grabbed our stuff. My mother and we children were waiting for him outside of the train—patiently but with nervous looks on our faces. Everybody was anticipating departing from the station before the sun went down and wondering what was next from there.

My stepfather got off the train and said, "Okay, let's see. Where do we go from here?" He looked around and thought about the best course of action. This was the last train stop in Sudan, so we could go no farther by train. Most of the people who got off the train left and got on some other sort of transportation. We stood there a while. It was slowly becoming dark, and we were the only people left at the train station. The train stood still as the engine slowly cooled off. We could see small mud-brick houses ahead of us. Finally, my stepfather and Mum came up with a plan. We did not know anybody at the new place, and my parents knew our condition very well.

"Let's go!" said my stepfather with a commanding presence in his voice. He grabbed Amoe's hand with his left hand and had a bag in his right. Mum had Makot on her arm. I walked alongside our parents as we trudged through the desert on foot to get to the houses we could see—perhaps ten miles away from the train station. We walked through the sandy Nubian landscape with no shoes on our feet. I sometimes had trouble keeping the pace and fell behind, but we all trudged on.

We arrived late in the night at the traditional mud-brick buildings that we saw earlier. Everyone in town was sleeping except for the few dogs barking at us. The small town had sand streets and no roads at all. We felt a laid-back vibe coming at us from the nice breeze flowing from Lake Nassar, or maybe it was just us who were laid back after a tiring journey. We reached a huge compound, and my stepfather went and asked for a big favor.

My mother and we children waited patiently for him to return with good news; never mind that we were nervous. My stepfather knocked on the door of a family we did not know, but in Sudanese culture, we could ask for a place to stay for the night since we did not have a place to sleep. The old man who answered the door appeared to be very friendly, and he conversed with my stepfather.

The old man was interested in our trip and was happy to be the first to welcome us warmly to Wadi Halfa, a relatively small town off the shore of Lake Nasser in the northernmost part of Sudan. We accepted his offer of hospitality and walked into a huge courtyard.

It was a big compound, and our host was a kind, elderly man and his family. He offered a room for us to stay in that night. The room was too hot and stuffy to sleep in comfortably, so my stepfather pulled the bed out to the courtyard area, and we slept there. Mum and my little sibling used the bed, and the rest of us used the blankets that came with us and slept on the floor. It was like any other night sleeping under the stars in Sudan, but this time we were strangers in the Nubian Desert. It was the first time in a long time for all of us to eat and sleep in a house. In the morning, we were treated to lots of tea and conversation; and at noon, we were treated to a great big meal with fish. The old man spoke Arabic and Dinka fluently.

The small, dusty town of Wadi Halfa is the point of entry into Sudan from Egypt. It was surrounded by the golden dunes of the Nubian Desert, the eastern edge of the Sahara, and had a population of less than 16,000. The first few days we were there, I saw the remaining pyramids, which predate the giant pyramids in Egypt. My stepfather told me Nubians were oppressed like the South Sudanese, with their history and ours intertwined. Historically, Wadi Halfa was Nubia's most significant trading point and was the gateway between Sudan and our neighbor country, Egypt. The buildings in Wadi Halfa were immaculate. It went from its glorious days as a thriving kingdom to a stereotypical border town, small and full of papers and plastic bags flying around.

The original Wadi Halfa was submerged when the famous Aswan High Dam created Lake Nasser in 1971. Sudan's military regime forcibly got rid of the natives from their lands and relocated them to the middle of the desert where access to water and food was difficult. Many died from malaria, other diseases, starvation, and thirst, particularly women, children, and elders. Those who refused to be relocated were brutally killed by the Islamic regime.

A few Nubians, however, managed to remain along the Nile. They were not going anywhere and were willing to die defending their land from government forces. A few of the brave ones who fought remained there since they believed that the River Nile built their ancestors' identities as fishermen and river traders. They built new settlements several times and finally settled on the current Wadi Halfa location when the flooding stopped. Seasonal flooding happens quite often, and it wipes out many residents when the river overflows.

The Nubian homeland, the area of southern Egypt and northern Sudan, has one of the harshest climates on Earth. The temperature is high through most of the year, and rainfalls are infrequent. The banks of the Nile are narrow in much of Nubia, which makes farming difficult. Yet, in antiquity, Nubia was a green land of great natural wealth, such as gold, ebony, ivory, and incense, which was always prized by her neighbor countries. Historically, Nubia is the homeland of Africa's earliest black culture with a rich history that can be traced back many centuries.

After a week, we left Wadi Halfa, Sudan, behind us and crossed the border to Aswan, Egypt, via a twenty-four-hour ferry ride across Lake Nasser. It was around 5:00 p.m. when we reached this small thriving city in the south of Egypt. My siblings and I complained about being hungry and found a small area that served food, which was surprisingly inexpensive. My stepfather put in a food order for the family. It was similar to Sudanese dishes—lamb and okra stew with Egyptian bread called aish baladi. We were amazed how tasty the food was and how similar to our own cooking style, perhaps because the people in Aswan are Nubian and not Arab Egyptians.

Aswan is a very beautiful and unique place. It was a very bustling city, probably because it is an important trading route. Another thing that caught our attention was the diversity of the people. Many of the people whom we saw in Aswan were not Arabs but descendants of the Nubian Kingdom or, simply put, ancient Egyptians. They were the descedants of the black pharaohs who conquered and ruled

Egypt and Sudan for centuries. These people were in fact Sudanese, and it is here where the black civilization began.

The ancient Egyptians called this place Swen and considered Aswan to be not only the end of the world but also the sacred source of the Nile. Its granite was used to build most of their temples that still stand today. For centuries, Aswan was the gateway to Africa and the land of Nubia, considered one of the earliest inhabited lands in the world. The Copts called it Souan, which means "trade," from which the present-day Aswan is derived. It was in Aswan where caravans came to trade camels, gold, and ivory in the established markets. The trading diminished with the infiltration of the Islamic people. Due to its strategic location, Aswan was chosen as the first capital of Upper Egypt, and the Ptolemies used it as a base to enter Nubia, Sudan, and Central Africa. It was they who built the beautiful Temple of Philae. Throughout history, from the time of the pharaohs to Muslim rule, governments sent troops to Aswan to protect Egypt from any southern invasions.

My family stayed in Aswan, Egypt's most culturally diverse ancient city, for only one day. The next day, we continued our long journey by train to Cairo. During our thirteen-hour train ride, we passed through Kom Ombo, Oedu, Luxor, Asyut, and Giza, places filled with historic wonders. The views from the train window were fascinating, especially along the Nile River. The train journey gave us an insight into a country that was historically part of Sudan but that we'd never seen before. Of course, we were nervous yet fascinated by the most fabulous ancient cities in the world. Our fascination with Egypt did not last long.

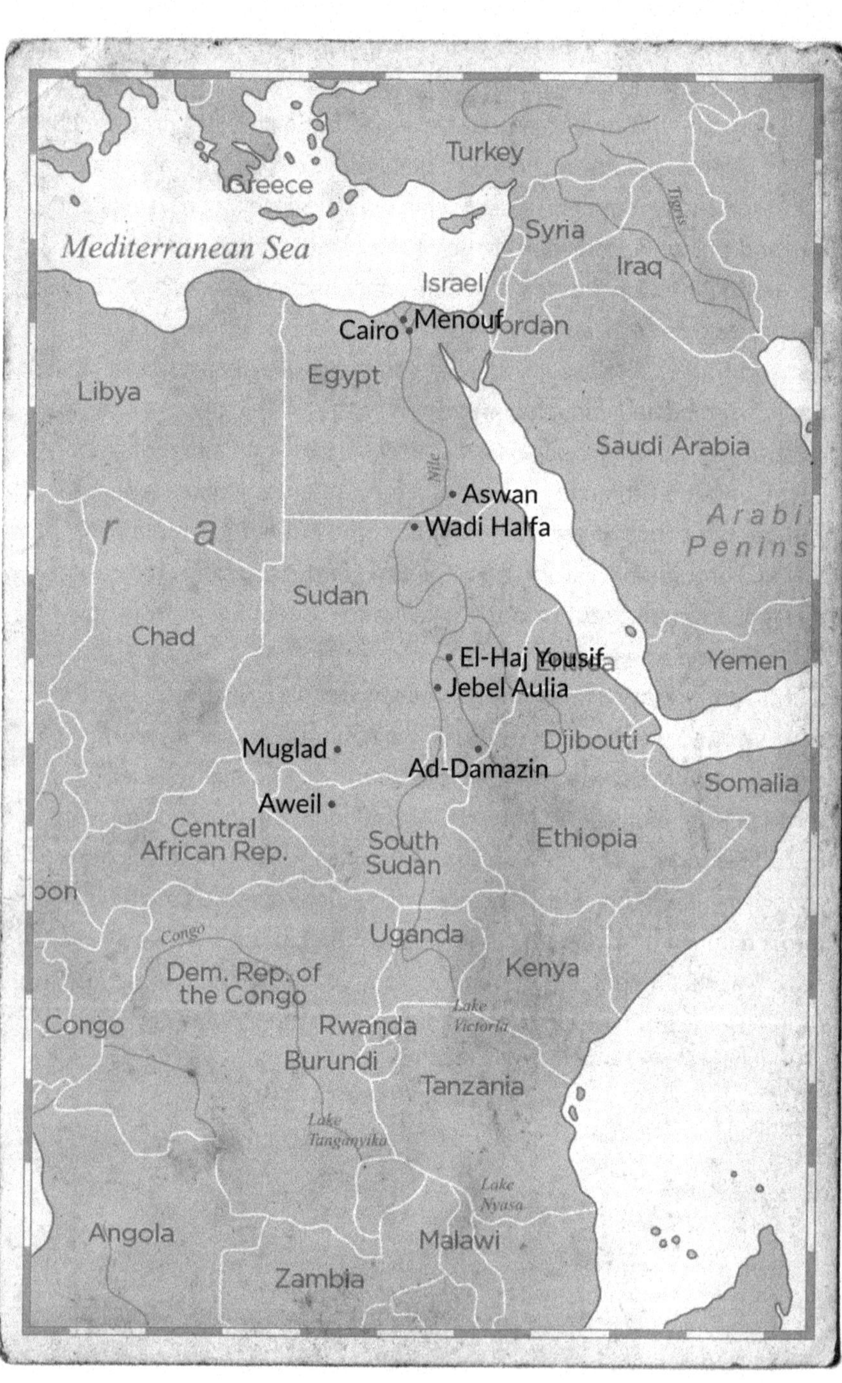

Mediterranean Sea
Greece
Turkey
Syria
Israel
Iraq
Tigris
Jordan
Cairo
Menouf
Egypt
Libya
Nile
Saudi Arabia
Aswan
Wadi Halfa
Arabi
Penins
Sudan
Chad
El-Haj Yousif
Jebel Aulia
Yemen
Muglad
Ad-Damazin
Djibouti
Somalia
Aweil
Central
African Rep.
South
Sudan
Ethiopia
oon
Congo
Uganda
Kenya
Dem. Rep. of
the Congo
Lake
Victoria
Congo
Rwanda
Burundi
Tanzania
Lake
Tanganyika
Lake
Nyasa
Angola
Malawi
Zambia

CHAPTER 4

Hostile Refuge

**She is clothed with strength
and dignity; she can laugh
at the days to come.**

– Proverbs 31:25 (NIV)

Egyptians refer to their country as Umm al-Dunya, meaning "mother of the world" in Arabic. The country that is referred to as "mother" did not offer our family a safe haven when we settled there as refugees in 1997. When we initially arrived in Egypt, we lived in a United Nations refugee camp where life was difficult.

A kind family in Cairo knew of my family and offered to host us. So we traveled to Cairo and lived with Zuber and his family in the Maadi district. Mr. Zuber was from the same Luo ethnic group as my family, and my stepfather knew him during their short time in Libya. The plan was to live with our host family until one of my parents found a decent job, probably within a month, and then we would move to our own apartment. In the meantime, Zuber and his wife would help my parents become familiar with places like church, the community centers, schools, and where to find employment. Due to my stepfather's health condition, this plan did not go well.

The economic crisis in Egypt made living conditions even harder. South Sudanese refugees faced discrimination on the streets of Cairo, workplace harassment, and police brutality. Refugees were not welcome.

To the Egyptians, my mother was just another uneducated African woman who could neither read nor write Arabic, one with children and an ill husband who would soon need medical attention in a foreign land. She found herself in Cairo, the second-largest city in Africa. From the start, the odds were against her. Egypt was not like living in Aweil, South Sudan, nor was it like living in displacement camps in Sudan.

Prior to coming to Egypt, my stepfather had an injury as a result of a beating by Sudanese police. In addition, he'd had a heart condition since he was a young man. In our first week in Egypt, my stepfather began to complain about chest pain followed by a high fever and coughing up blood and mucus. His health seemed to worsen every minute. Mr. Zuber called a taxi, and my stepfather was taken to a nearby hospital for treatment. After a chest X-ray and blood tests at the hospital, he was diagnosed with tuberculosis. Tuberculosis is caused by *Mycobacterium tuberculosis* and most commonly affects the lungs but can also affect other areas of the body. We hoped we would be able to see my stepfather within a few days, but he ended up being hospitalized for much longer. The doctors discovered from the X-rays that my stepfather had several deep holes in his lungs that needed serious medical attention.

We visited my stepfather during that third week he was at the hospital. During our visit, we saw how weak he was and worried he was not going to survive another day. His eyes were open, but he was unable to recognize us. He could not speak because he had a tube in his mouth that assisted him with breathing. A mechanical ventilator next to his bed controlled the volume and duration of breath throughout the respiration cycle. The doctor told Mr. Zuber that my stepfather would be transferred to another hospital called Menoufia University Hospital located in the northern part of Egypt near the

Nile Delta. Mr. Zuber translated that to my mother since she could not speak Arabic. The new hospital was three to four hours away from Maadi where we lived. I remember the silence as we sat near the hospital bed. It was sad to see my stepfather wrapped up with white sheets and his hands tied to the bed so that he wouldn't pull the tube from his mouth. This image and long silence were not easy to digest as we watched his chest rise and fall with each breath.

Back at the apartment where we lived, things were not going well financially. My mother gave the last bit of money we had to support our host family with rent, food, electricity, and water. Another family that recently fled to Egypt had joined us, and the tiny apartment became overcrowded with a total of three families. Like most South Sudanese refugees in Cairo, we shared apartments to defray the cost of rent, but the overcrowding led to problems between the refugees and Egyptian landlords. The increased rent price was the major problem, and it had burdened the families we lived with. Frustration began to set in as life got tougher in the foreign land with no assistance from any organization. Three weeks after we arrived in Egypt, our host family was already behind on their bills. As a result, the landlord came by and kicked everybody out on the street. This was a nightmare and an unbelievable experience! The families scattered and went their separate ways to the camps.

Mother found herself homeless with three children and a hospitalized husband. My family had lived in Egypt for less than a month, and we went from living in a crowded apartment to homelessness with a blink of an eye. It was terrifying, of course. Thankfully, we managed not to end up on the street. Instead, my mother took us to the church where we joined other homeless South Sudanese refugees who did not know anybody and could not afford to rent an apartment. As a homeless family, the Sacred Heart Parish Catholic Church in Cairo (also known as *Kanesia Sakakini* in Arabic) became our shelter for the next four months.

The Sacred Heart Parish has been serving the refugee and displaced South Sudanese community living in Cairo since 1984.

At the church, regular worship services are held in both Arabic and English, and Christian educational programs for all age groups are offered for the community to attend. The church is a cultural community center for the refugees. The church also offered educational, health, and cultural programs for all in the refugee community from all faiths, so upon resettlement, their opportunities for a successful transition might be enhanced and South Sudanese cultural heritage preserved.

Despite the helping hand the church extended to make life tolerable to the community, life in Egypt remained difficult. Even though the church served as our shelter, which was far better than living on the streets of Cairo, it was still not a home, and living there came with daily restrictions. For example, the church gate had to be shut by a certain time. If you were not in by that time, you would spend the night on the street. And only two restrooms were available. My family waited until everybody was out of the church compound to take care of hygiene.

We had to be up early in the morning to take care of bathroom needs, pack our stuff, and put them away before school started. In short, everything we did was not on our own timetable. My mother had to walk to a friend's apartment, cook, and then bring back the food. Since church served as a community center, refugees came there to socialize, relax, and take breaks from the headaches that came with living in Egypt. For a homeless family like ours, bedtime was determined by how fast the other refugees left to go to their apartments. In case you did not know, South Sudanese people love to talk—a lot. In one corner, young men would be flirting with young women. In the other, a group of elders would be talking politics and sharing their grievances about the horrific civil war that had ravaged Sudan for more than thirty years. In the midst of all this, you couldn't miss the loud noise from children running around having fun and just being kids.

South Sudanese parents recognized the difficulties their children faced in accessing education. As a result, parents and volunteer teachers established a school for refugee children. The school house was in the same church compound where we resided. Education was not free, so Mum had to borrow some money to make sure my siblings and I were registered. Even though we were homeless, my mother's expectations were high and left no room for excuses. She encouraged us to strive for excellence in school. Each night, Mum would tell us that we needed our school uniforms ready and our shoes next to the clothes because she did not want any problems in the morning. She usually had to deal with some of us who struggled to wake up early. In the morning, she would inspect us to make sure we looked presentable. Upon her approval, we were expected to be first at the formation where attendance was taken.

At the morning formation, we sang the Sudanese national anthem with our right hands placed on our hearts. I can't speak for my siblings, but I knew that I did not know all the words for the national anthem, so I stood there looking good and mumbled through to the end. Afterward, we were dismissed to go to our classes in a single file. The teachers did not waste time, and we were issued books on the first day of school. There weren't enough books to go around, so three students shared each book. When school ended, the students with whom I shared the book and I could not decide who should keep the book. The first day of school went pretty fast, and we met new friends. The school did not provide lunch, so we went "home" with empty stomachs. By home, I mean the corner of the church where we resided. This was our first taste of school life as refugees in Egypt.

During school hours, a kid my age asked a question that I remember vividly. He approached me during lunch break and asked, "Does your family live here at church by the corner near the metal storage cage?" "Yes, we do," I sincerely replied. The kids were curious to know why a group of poor families, including my own, lived at the church. One day after school, I was tired, sleepy, and hungry. I went to rest under a huge, wooden concert stage that was set up at the church for an upcoming event. While I was resting, my brother Amoe joined me, and we ended up sleeping underneath it because it was the only area with shade. By the time we awoke, several South Sudanese kids were staring and laughing at us. They were laughing at us because they thought that they were "above us" since they lived in their own apartments. The truth is, homelessness can happen to any South Sudanese refugee in Egypt. What those kids failed to realize was that their families could be the next group living in the same corner. No refugee was totally immune to harsh economic conditions and Egypt's skyrocketing unemployment. Life in Egypt was miserable!

South Sudanese refugees were forced to overcome much more serious problems than native Egyptians because the majority of refugees did not have proper documents. As a result, they were forced into the "dark economy," which pushed them to work illegally at cafes, on construction sites, and other manual jobs where abuse was routine with little legal protection. The church had a program that assisted the refugees in finding jobs, but the process often took months. My mother registered as soon as she discovered that the program existed. She explained our situation, speaking in Dinka, the dialect that she spoke fluently, and it was translated into Arabic: "I am a mother of three children, and my husband has been hospitalized since we arrived four months ago. Currently, I reside here at the church and do not speak Arabic. My family is not in great condition. Could you assist me in finding a job?" Her name made it on the urgent list for those who needed a job right away. Two weeks later, a tall, thin Dinka gentleman came with the news that they had found a job for her. Legal employment in Egypt was nearly impossible for South Sudanese refugees, and thankfully Mum took advantage of the program that the church offered. My mother's first job in Egypt was in the informal economy as a domestic worker for an Egyptian family where she worked long hours to make ends meets. When she got her first pay check, she paid the school fees for all of us.

At the first opportunity, my mother took the family to go see my stepfather in the hospital. His health hadn't improved much, and he was a long way from being discharged. We noticed that he was alone and segregated from other patients at the hospital. Mum told my stepfather that we no longer lived at the apartment and lived at the church instead.

"Don't worry. I recently got a job, and things will get better," she told him. My stepfather looked worried, but she assured him. "Don't stress over our situation. We will get out of it soon." My stepfather felt hopeless about how things turned out, but my Mum assured him that things would get better, that she was working and saving to rent our own apartment.

"How are they treating you?" Mum asked.

"I have been assigned an American doctor. He is a great doctor," my stepfather stated.

"That's great, and I am happy to hear that," said Mum. "What kind of medication are they giving you?"

"Pain medication every six hours and medication for breathing," he said.

Hospital visiting hours were slowly closing in on us, so my mother pulled cash out of her purse and gave the money to my stepfather. "Here you go. This is for you in case you need extra money for medication and other things that you wish to buy while you are here."

After being in the hospital all day, we said goodbye to our stepfather and returned to Cairo. On our long return ride, I could sense that my mother was worried about my stepfather being lonely at the hospital. At that time, he was the only black patient in the entire hospital, and that often worried my mother because Egyptian nurses and doctors were known for organ trafficking, and South Sudanese refugees were often easy targets.

Upon returning to Cairo, my mother had to learn to speak Egyptian Arabic very fast. She mixed up a little Sudanese Arabic with Egyptian Arabic and was able to communicate to the best of her ability. That created an opportunity for her to get a second job as a babysitter for another Egyptian family who knew the family she was working for. In fact, her boss from the first job strongly recommended her for the position because the family admired her work ethic and honesty.

Every day, she went to work at 7 a.m. and returned to the church at 7 p.m. The two locations where she worked were far from each other, so when she was done with one job, she would take the bus to the other job. By the time she returned to the church, she was extremely exhausted. She made these sacrifices in order to put food on the table and to support her ill husband financially at the hospital. My mother worked hard, and slowly things were beginning to change course. Halfway into our fourth month of homelessness in Egypt, Mum dug our family out of that miserable life. By the time the new month rolled around, we packed up our belongings and walked out of the church with our heads held high. She had saved up enough money to put a roof over our heads!

We moved into a small, two-bedroom apartment at 15 Almardini Street, Deir Almalak, Cairo, Egypt. It was in a destitute neighborhood on the outskirts of Cairo but had running water, electricity, a phone, a stove, and a TV. A Sudanese lady who did not have a place to stay joined us and helped with rent. The lady was very helpful, and she stayed home with us when Mum was at work. Then one day I discovered that she was from the Dinka Agar ethnic group. Legend says the Agar people can turn into hyenas or lions. Imagine how terrified my siblings and I were!

Whenever Mum went to work, we made sure there was enough food in our bedroom before we locked ourselves in the room. One day, the lady came and knocked on our door to ask if we could come out and eat the food she kindly prepared for us. We refused to answer and kept the door shut! "My children, please come out and eat," she said. We kept quiet because we thought she was going eat us.

One weekend, my mother was home with the lady, so out of curiosity the lady asked my mother, "Why are your children afraid of me?" My younger brother innocently spoke the truth and told my mother that we were afraid because Agar people eat other people. Then she and my mother started to laugh out loud. "I apologize. I did not mean to scare you guys," she told us. From that point on, we discovered that the story was myth and not true. Thankfully, the lady did not feel offended.

***

In Egypt, organ trafficking was on the rise because criminals were making big profits from selling refugee body parts. The situation was nothing short of catastrophic for the South Sudanese as many lived on the streets and the majority had no access to basic resources or job prospects. The traffickers took advantage of the influx of refugees who were not protected by Egyptian law and convinced some to sell their body parts, which they did in desperation and in hopes of making money. But those who resorted to selling their body parts were few in number compared to other victims who are abducted for their organs. Egyptian church officials were overwhelmed by reports of heinous human rights violations that South Sudanese refugees faced in their daily lives. The United Nations was helpless as it drastically lacked the funds and staff to adequately address the needs of thousands of refugees organ trafficking victims.

When my stepfather was admitted to Menoufia University Hospital, he was the only black person among predominately Arab patients. The hospital is located in Menouf, one of the ancient Egyptian cities in the governorate. My stepfather was alone and far from Cairo, where we lived, which worried my mother. She took Amoe and me to live in Menouf with my stepfather at the hospital while she worked two jobs to support the family. The rooms at the hospital were divided into big sections with multiple beds. The room where my stepfather was assigned had six beds, one occupied by him. When my brother and I arrived, we took two available beds and lived there with him for several months.

I was ten years old and terrified by the horror stories of organ traffickers, which was a reality in Egyptian hospitals. I kept my eyes open and watched the door all night. I was a watchdog over my stepfather and sibling, so our organs wouldn't be stolen while we were asleep. While they slept, I walked around to check on them to make sure they were okay. I averaged four hours of sleep during the day and stayed up the entire night until the sun rose. The stress level and anxiety took a toll on me, and I lost a lot of weight.

My mother came to visit us at the hospital after the first month and immediately noticed how much I had changed. On the other hand, Amoe enjoyed hospital food and gained weight because his mind was free from worries. My stepfather and Amoe still do not know to this day that I sacrificed my sleep to protect them from harm. This was the biggest secret I ever kept as a child.

Aside from worries and nightmares I experienced while at the hospital, Menouf was a pretty quiet city. My stepfather took us for walks inside the hospital compound and watched us play on playground swings. These little moments helped me cope with life at the hospital.

Living at the hospital was like a prison for both my stepfather and me. One day, he told me that I did not have to eat the hospital food and that I was free to get food from nearby restaurants. I craved *ful medames*, my favorite Egyptian dish—fava beans cooked with vegetable oil, cumin, garlic, onion, lemon juice, herbs, and spices. I went outside the compound for the first time since I arrived in Menouf and was intrigued to know what the city was like outside the hospital walls.

I went to a restaurant and ordered food. As I waited in line, I noticed more people came near and started to stare at me. I tried to ignore them as I continued to wait. It seemed like the longer I was there, the more people came. Eventually, there were about thirty to forty people ranging from children and teens to women and men. These Egyptians were all intrigued by the color of my skin, white teeth, and hair, and my ability to speak Egyptian Arabic. It became clear to me that none of them had encountered a black human being in their lives. I was their first, and they wanted to see, hear, and feel if I was human. I vividly remember a few of them attempting to touch my skin, but I refused. A teenage girl asked if she could feel my hair. The answer she got was a no. Suddenly, a five-year-old boy was brave enough to get closer to me and rubbed his small fingers against my left arm. He then checked his fingers as others slowly watched for any black marks left on his fingers. They were amazed to see that my skin was not artificial as they thought, but real like theirs, only black. I got my food and left with many following me all the way to the doors of the hospital compound. When I got back to the room, I explained what happened to stepfather, and he told me that he had similar experiences.

There is a huge difference between Menouf and Cairo. The inhabitants of Menouf are farmers with little to no education. Their world is limited only to Menouf, and many have never traveled to other parts of their own country. Therefore, I was able to understand why they were curious seeing a black human being. The people were very peaceful for the most part, and I noticed no racist attitude. I only saw curiosity when I first interacted with these poor farmers. It reminded me of the time when kids my age in the displaced camp in Sudan were curious to touch white aid workers from Britain and America. My brother Maywal was among the brave kids who actually got close enough to touch a white person. On the other hand, I used to run away from white aid workers as a little boy because I had never seen such people in my life. My world was black, and I was never exposed to different human beings until I discovered from my mother that white people were people like us. We are all humans, and we are curious about new things, but unfortunately this world tends to portray certain human beings as lesser than others.

Life in Egypt for black people was not as beautiful and glorious as it was when ruled by the black pharaohs of the Nile in the glorious past. Blacks in Egypt were deemed "inferior," and that long-standing racism subjected them to varying degrees of discrimination and degradation on the streets of Cairo. The long-standing racist attitude toward black people threatened the security and livelihoods of my family and thousands of South Sudanese refugees in Egypt. A black woman like my mother could not purchase groceries or shop for food from the market but had tomatoes, oranges, and other objects thrown at her because of the color of her skin. My friends and I could not walk like normal human beings without water being poured on our heads from the balcony because we were black Africans. My mother and other women could not walk home safely after work without being harassed and called names. My stepfather could not comfortably be hospitalized in Egypt without having to worry about his body parts being removed illegally from his body by doctors who wanted to profit from disadvantaged refugees. Racial slurs were commonly directed toward black people in public places every day. The terms *chocalata* and *samara* are often used as racial slurs to refer to black people. The terms *zarboon* and *hungia-bongia* mean "big, black gorilla." In Egypt's hierarchy, all black people are ranked to the level of *abade* meaning "slave" in Arabic.

To this day, there is no day in Cairo where a black person is free from being called a slave or having objects thrown at them. Life is a struggle for all South Sudanese in Cairo, especially for women who are often victims of sexual assault and harassment at the work place. Black women are often assumed to be promiscuous. They are often treated as concubines by Egyptian men whom they worked for and on the streets by random males.

Strong African women like my mother and her friends worked over eighty hours weekly to make ends meets. They were neither concubines nor prostitutes who wanted monies from Egyptian men. Instead, they were strong and faithful women who were married with children. They were the backbones of their families and worked hard to earn every single penny to put food on the table, yet they were victims of sexual harassment and racial discrimination in Egypt.

I have no doubt that the media influences racism in modern-day Egypt. The representation of black people in movies and other media outlets has often historically been either marginal or racist at its highest level. Black men are often cast as doormen, guards, cooks, servants, and taxi drivers, while black women are often portrayed as the maid or the nanny. The Egyptian news media criminalizes the black community. For example, Egyptian newspapers openly and falsely accused black teenagers and described them as "terror gangs" who committed crimes across the country. This fabricated news allowed the police to harass black people who were found walking on the street, rounding them up and subjecting them to police brutality.

Beautiful, tall, and dark-skinned South Sudanese women walking on streets of Cairo with their thick, kinky hair often woven uniquely in braids, are routinely the targets of verbal public abuse. When young South Sudanese girls walked home from school, truckloads of Arab Egyptian men would drive by hanging out of the windows, shouting catcalls, and making loud demands for sexual favors. One day my sister Amal and I were walking home from school, and three Egyptian men approached us and began calling us all kinds of names. I told them if any of them laid their hands on my sister, I would cut their throats in a heartbeat and send them to Allah! I picked up rocks to warn them. They shied away because it was obvious that I was serious, and they saw other South Sudanese men headed our way. I was eleven years old at the time, but I roared like a lion! I was not afraid of them. My brothers and I are very protective of our sister, but I was more aggressive than all of them. I was always protective of my sister regardless of whether it was a South Sudanese man who might be interested in her or a stranger who wanted to harm her.

In my experience, Arab Egyptians do not like sub-Saharan Africans—period. Racism infects all aspects of Egyptian life, much as it does in America. I was not shocked to learn that more than a few Arab Egyptians disliked their dark-skinned former President Anwar Sadat. President Anwar Sadat was born in Al-Minufiyyah, Egypt, to a poor Nubian family and later rose to become the third president of Egypt from October 15, 1970, until his assassination by Islamic fundamentalists on October 6, 1981. During his presidency, President Sadat faced insults by his Arab Egyptian population in Egypt who insisted that he "did not look Egyptian enough" because of the color of his skin and his Sudanese heritage. The president's mother was a

Sudanese Nubian, and he had been ridiculed for years as "Nasser's black poodle." This racially fueled term was used to refer to his skin color by those who did not like him when he served under President Gamal Adel Nasser as vice president. Arabs in general did not like the idea of having a person of color in power.

Over the years that we lived in Egypt, I came to the realization that the majority of Egyptians do not consider themselves Africans, but rather Arabs. Many Egyptians take offense to being identified with Africa in any way, shape, or form. They associate themselves with the Arab world despite the fact that Egypt is on the African continent geographically. It's true that the vast population of present-day Arabs are not Africans. Historically speaking, Egypt's history has always been close to Sudan and that of black African civilization, which modern day Arab Egyptians try to exclude themselves from. For too many Arab Egyptians, sub-Saharan Africa is a stereotypical exotic region of thick jungles inhabited by multitudes of poor, starving and black-skinned "savages." I find that ironic because I have seen homeless and starving Arab Egyptians around Cairo who are no different from any other Africans who are starving any place on the African continent.

As far as black skin is concerned, real Egyptians are in fact descendants of black people of Nubia and other ethnicities that occupied Sudan and Egypt before Arabs came with their Islamic ideology and occupied the land that once belonged to the Sudanese Nubians. From our journey, we learned that South Sudanese refugees were oppressed in Egypt because of racial and religious affiliation, which were among the reasons that forced them to flee from Sudan in the first place. As a small boy, I saw injustice, inequality, religious persecution, and police brutality. Despite all the difficulty, my mother stayed positive in the face of these challenges the family endured. My mother hoped that the war would end sooner rather than later, so we could return to Sudan. Unfortunately, that hope never materialized for our family. The Almighty God had a different plan for our family!

The corner at the Sacred Heart Parish Catholic Church in Cairo, Egpyt, where the Maywal family resided for several months while homeless. *Photo courtesy of Marlin Maywal.*

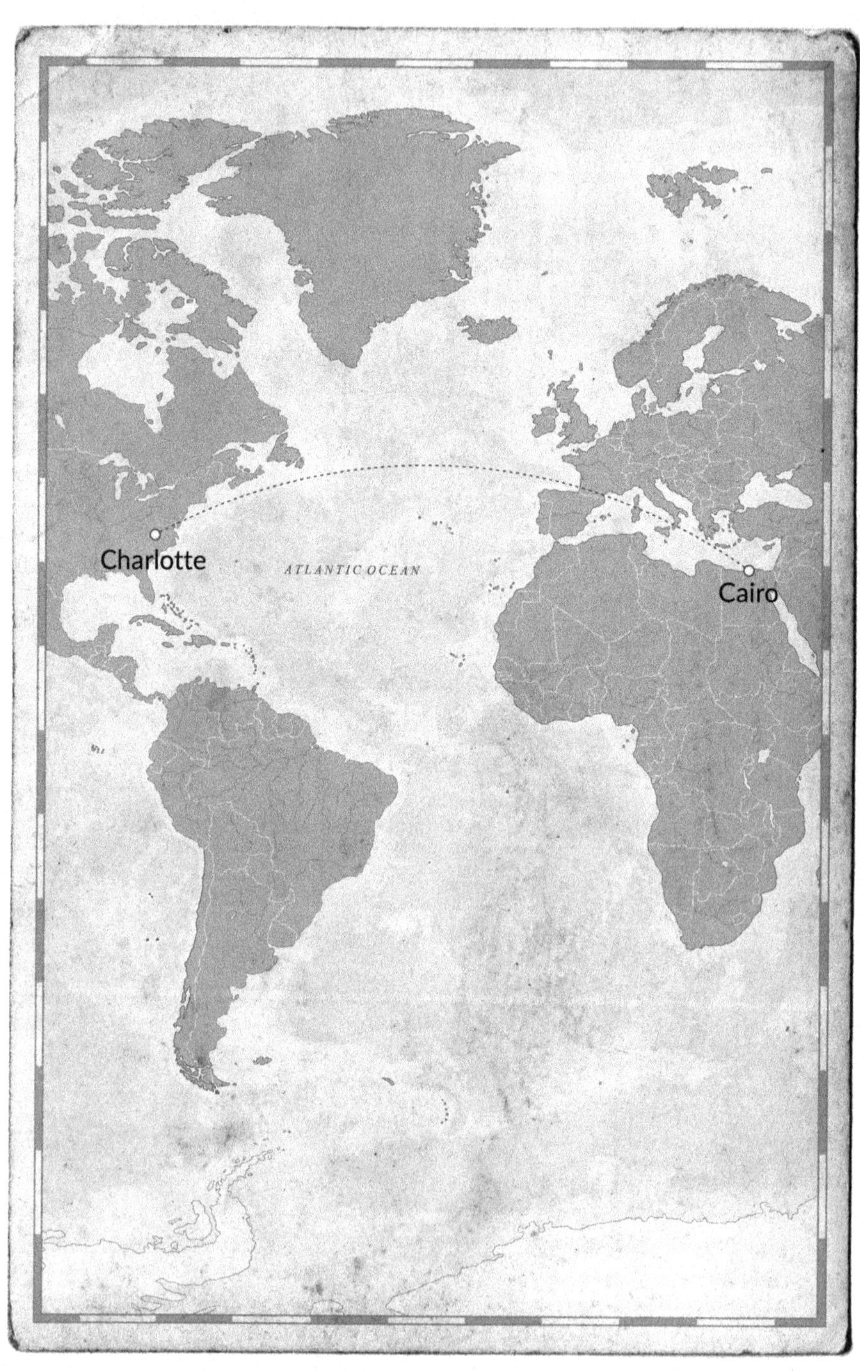

Charlotte
ATLANTIC OCEAN
Cairo

CHAPTER 5

The Shores of Freedom

**My fellow Americans, we are and
always will be a nation of immigrants.
We were strangers once, too.**

– President Barack Obama, remarks by the president
in an address to the nation on immigration

Life in Egypt was horrible, to say the least, and the war continued in Sudan. When my family escaped Sudanese civil war for Egypt, we hoped for a better life. My mother was very homesick for the children she had left at the displacement camp in Sudan. Finally, Allah-jabo, Amal, and Maywal were able to leave the displacement camp and join us in Egypt. Only Aketch remained in the displacement camp, with her family, and her life would take a different path as time went by.

In 2000, my mother learned from her friends that the United Nation High Commissioner for Refugees (UNHCR) was taking applications to resettle thousands of refugees to any country that would accept them. The opportunity to leave Egypt for a better life in the West gave hope to many of the refugees, including my family. To my knowledge, all the South Sudanese refugees that made it to Egypt applied for refugee status with the UNHCR. My mother reviewed our condition in Egypt, which was miserable at the time. She worked two jobs to provide for the family and had a husband who had been hospitalized since we arrived in Egypt.

My mother wanted a better life for her children. She envisioned her children getting the best education and her ill husband getting the best treatment. She wanted to escape the struggle in Egypt and the civil war in Sudan. She believed that a better life and a brighter future for her family would be in America. So she applied to UNHCR to immigrate to America because America has the best doctors, nurses, hospitals, and medical breakthrough medicines in the world. Mum had help filling out the application from a Sudanese gentleman who wrote down everything she could remember when she fled her village. She was called for an interview three months later. She stood before the UN board members and told them her story through an interpreter, about how her village came under attack and the 500-mile journey she took on foot to reach the displacement camp in northern Sudan. She shared the fear of being persecuted for being Christian by the Islamic regime that killed 2.5 million people, including some of her family members, in an attempt to create an Islamic state in Sudan. After her interview, she called my stepfather to let him know that she had applied with UNHCR to resettle in America.

After my mother went for her first interview, her application was reviewed by UNHCR in order to declare if my family was deemed "refugee." By UNHCR's definition, a refugee is one who is "owing to a well-founded fear of being persecuted for reasons of race, religion, nationality, membership of a particular social group or political opinion, is outside the country of his nationality, and is unable to, or owing to such fear, is unwilling to avail himself/herself of the protection of that country" (UNHCR 1951). We undoubtedly fit the UN definition of refugees. My mother was the author of that story. At this point, my mother had done everything she could to give our family hope of a better life ahead. Now, the only thing she could do was to pray and wait for her application to be granted or rejected for resettlement. The process can take up two years before results are announced. During the period of waiting, my mother put everything in

God's hands. We knew that the result of her prayers and application would have a profound impact and fundamentally change our lives for better or worse.

Every night before we went to bed, my mother would always pray with us by asking the Almighty God to open the gate to a brighter future. In our deepest and darkest moments, what really got our family through those difficult days in Egypt was my mother's prayers. Sometimes her prayer was, "God, help protect my children as they walk to school without my presence. Be there for them as they return from school." Sometimes her prayer was, "Watch over my children's father at the hospital and protect him as he continues with medical treatment." My mother's prayers were often in the Dinka dialect, which we all understood. Sometimes she prayed in her Luo dialect. Her prayers were very powerful, and we were often moved by them. The intimate connection and spiritual communication with Almighty God were what got us through everything despite the circumstances. Mum taught us that God's support and miracles are just a prayer away, if our faith is strong.

Finally, after waiting for over a year, my brother Allah-jabo happened to be at the church. He walked over to the board where names of families that were granted resettlement to Western countries were posted. He looked at the list and saw "Adout Goi," my mother's name, on the list of those who had been approved to resettle in the United States of America. Next to my mother's name was "Principal Applicant," which meant that she was the head of the case for our family. My brother could not believe his eyes! He could not believe that we were US bound within the next forty-eight hours. Allah-jabo took off from the church and ran home to share the good news. When he arrived, he was sweating and was very excited. "We have forty-eight hours to pack our stuff. We are going to America! I saw your name, Mum, on the list!" said Allah-jabo. My mother did not believe it, so she got dressed and went to the church with Allah-jabo to confirm with church officials who worked with the United Nations. It was confirmed and was a dream come true. When they both returned, we did not waste time. "We are going to America," my siblings and I shouted as we danced around cheering in our excitement! We packed all day.

My mother's refugee application was then processed by a Resettlement Support Center. During the application process, after my mother was interviewed, the entire family went through an intensive screening process that included another interview, a medical evaluation and an inter-agency security screening process. The process is meant to ensure that the refugees do not pose any threat to the United States. Agencies involved in that vetting process included the Department of Homeland Security, the Defense Department, the State Department, and the Federal Bureau of Investigation. These agencies conducted background checks on all of us, fingerprinted us, and looked up our names to make sure we were not on the list of terrorists or people who are banned by the US government from entering the country. During the final interview, my mother was asked by the security official, "Do you swear to tell the truth, the whole truth, and nothing but the truth so help you God?" "Yes," she replied. The security officials asked each of us children the same questions they asked of the adults. It did not matter whether a child or an adult knew the meaning of the word "treason" or "communist." The fact that we were minors did not matter; we were still subjected to security questions. My family successfully passed the high-level security clearance portion with no problem since we were poor, innocent refugees with no criminal backgrounds and no association to governments or terrorist groups that were hostile toward the United States.

For a long time, my mother did not expect her family to be approved for refugee status and referred to the United States. However, she put everything in God's hands and waited for the miracle to unfold before her eyes. Coming to America—this place of opportunity and freedom she once heard of—felt like a pipe dream, but with God's blessing, her vision became a reality. When the UN official at the church told Mum that her family was authorized to go to Charlotte, North Carolina, unexpected emotions fell over the family. We were excited about a new home in this amazing country called America that everybody spoke of, and we did not have guilt for leaving Sudan, Egypt, or all of Africa behind us. We had first stayed at the UN refugee camp, then we were homeless in a corner of the church courtyard, and then we lived in a shabby, one-bedroom apartment during our last year in Cairo. My family had nothing when we lived in Egypt.

For generations, America has served as a beacon of hope for many. In March 2001, our family (Mum, stepfather, Allah-jabo, Amal, Maywal, Amoe, Makot, and me), who had never been on an airplane before in our lives, got on an airplane to leave Egypt to come to a place called the United States of America. My mother had heard great things about America but had never seen it. There was no Internet then to search for this land that was so far and so great. She heard the legend that there was a place on this planet where the people were free, and the door of opportunity was open to all who reached the shores of freedom. When our plane took off from Cairo International Airport, we knew that we were not simply coming to a geographical place; we were coming to a country ranked first among a community of nations. Ideas such as freedom, justice, and equality abound for all. There was a lot to love about America: freedom, liberty, the melting pot of diversity, individualism—all democratic principles that attract people from all walks of life who had never lived under a democratic government. Our family had experienced civil war, homelessness, and absolute poverty that can crush the human soul, but we were all starting a new chapter in our lives—in America.

On March 13, 2001, as our plane began to descend at John F. Kennedy International Airport, we were amazed to view one of the world's most famous landmarks, the Statue of Liberty. It stood out then, as it had for so many immigrants arriving before us, as an iconic symbol of the United States and freedom for us. We were blessed to have come to the US through New York City and were able to see the beauty of America at first sight. It was an incredible moment and a memorable experience for us and other new arrivals. We could not wait for our plane to touch down and be able to see more of America on the ground.

Once our plane landed, we departed JFK International Airport to go to a nearby hotel where we stayed for the night. On our way to the hotel, we continued to see and embrace the beauty of America through the car window. We saw tall skyscrapers, busy streets with cars, and beautiful bridges with glowing lights. The most fascinating thing we noticed immediately about New York was the diversity of the people from all walks of life. It was obvious that New York is a city that never sleeps. It was a busy and beautiful city both from above and on the ground.

We returned to the airport the next day, and it was extremely cold. Not used to the cold temperatures, we were all shivering and looking forward to a warmer place. Even though we brought jackets from Egypt, those jackets could not keep us warm! We flew out of New York City on March 14, 2001, bound for the great state of North Carolina.

We arrived at our final destination, Charlotte, North Carolina, around 4 p.m. Our family was picked up from Charlotte Douglas International Airport by our sponsor, Ms. Fonk. On our way "home," she made a quick stop at McDonald's to purchase dinner for our family. It was surprising to discover that America was not only the land of the free but also the home of fast food restaurants. After arriving, we discovered that we had truly picked the right place to live because of the outpouring of support from the community. David McGoldrick and his wonderful wife and children brought us boxes of cereal, juice, cookies, chips, and water. Nuns from the Catholic church brought us clothes, shoes, bed sheets, pillows, and blankets. Mr. Sabet, a former South Sudanese refugee from Equatoria, brought us milk, bananas, soda, bread, and rice. Other people prepared hot food for us to eat. The welcome and generosity from strangers was overwhelming. They helped us settle in our new home at 1344 Green Oaks Lane, Apartment K.

It did not take us long to realize that our neighbors were refugees from Vietnam, Somalia, Bosnia, and Sudan. Our family was the fourth South Sudanese family to arrive in the community. The only non-refugee residents at our apartment complex were black Americans, and they did not have much in common with the rest of the residents. We refugees had a lot in common with each other, despite not speaking the same language. The kids got together to play soccer in the field between the apartment buildings while parents sat on the front porch to enjoy the game. In some ways, the life of the refugees in this small community was no different from the refugee camps in their respective countries. The biggest difference was the fact that conditions had changed from extreme poverty to better conditions with access to food, clean water, electricity, health care, and freedom. From my own observation, I would say the majority of refugees, including my family, were grateful and happy to be in the United States of America.

The only way to know what America was really like was to go out and meet new people. One of my brothers and I took a walk around our complex in an attempt to get a feel for our new environment. At once, we were curious to interact with three black American kids. They looked African to us, and they sounded like they were speaking an African dialect. They were riding their bicycles around. Then they stopped and started talking to each other. We were excited to start our first conversation and make new friends. We went up to them and asked, "What tribe are you from?" We got silence, a stare, and a question to the effect of "WTF did you just say?" We exchanged a friendly laugh among ourselves. They laughed at us, and we laughed at them. We departed after our encounter due to the language barrier. What we thought sounded like an African dialect was actually slang words that they used to communicate among themselves. This was definitely a "we (Africans) meet black Americans" experience for us.

Long before we arrived in the US, we had heard about black Americans. We knew that they were the offspring of millions of Africans who were pushed through the door of no return against their will. They were shipped from places such as Elmina and Ghana into lives of forced slavery in countries like Brazil, the Caribbean, and America. Today, scholars are not even sure of the number of Africans stolen from their land and forced into slavery, but the number lies between 10 and 28 million. These Africans were believed to have been shipped across the mighty Atlantic Ocean between the fifteenth and nineteenth centuries (Ryan 2017). Through their journey, many died on the way, and those who made it endured a life of drudgery working on tobacco, sugar, and cotton plantations. The way the first Africans made it to America was extremely worse compared to the way we arrived in America.

My siblings and I explored our new country and learned about this new society through new friends we made at school. My younger brothers and I attended Crown Point Elementary School, while my two older siblings attended Eastway Middle School. At school, we wondered why Americans loved to smile so much. We found this to be very awkward behavior because we thought there was no way someone could be happy all the time. It's impossible! We learned that friendliness is a huge cultural cornerstone in American culture, especially the South. Therefore, we learned to be friendly, even to strangers. In our South Sudanese culture, people smile when they are happy. Therefore, smiles are reserved for expressing genuine emotion and happiness. For us who were new at the time, we could not tell whether our American friends' smiles were genuine or not. Of course, Americans smile to indicate a friendly, cooperative nature as well. However, that was something that took time for us to understand.

Making eye contact was another strange behavior to us. In South Sudanese culture, when children speak to adults, they are expected not to make eye contact with their elders. This practice is similar in most African cultures because it shows the relationship between a junior and a senior. The minor is expected to keep their face down as a sign of respect. Therefore, making eye contact with an adult was considered disrespectful. At school, I had trouble adapting to this new way, and I remember vividly how absurd it was. At one point, my teacher asked me to step outside the classroom and asked me if I had done my homework. I lowered my face and told him yes. He said, "Look at me when I speak to you, Bol." He asked multiple times, and my answer was the same. Eventually, I politely raised my head and looked directly in his eyes and told him that it was out of respect that I spoke with my face down, and it was not because I lied. I had no reason to lie, but making eye contact while speaking to an adult was something new to me. By the end of this discussion, both of us learned something about each other.

My mother was very appreciative of the opportunity to escape the harsh conditions in Africa and come to the land of the brave and home of the free. Folks would think that struggles faced by refugees like my family would end as soon as we arrived in America. Right? That was certainly not the case for my family because we were faced with many obstacles once we arrived in the US. My parents had difficulty speaking and learning English. They had difficulty completing even basic tasks, such as buying food or filling out job applications. To help with this, my mother attended English as a second language (ESL) classes, and even that was difficult because she had never gone to school in Sudan. To make our situation even more difficult, my stepfather became ill again. He was seen at the hospital, and the doctor told Mum he needed surgery as soon as possible. He was admitted to the hospital for few days, and his left lung was removed to save the right lung that was not affected. The holes the doctors in Egypt had seen had spread all over his left lung. Three days after surgery, he came home and had to be on a ventilator. The doctors told my mother that my stepfather had three years to live. This was our first bad news in America.

My stepfather couldn't work because he was medically disabled. Mum had two months to find a job and provide for the family. Imagine her situation. But she who could not speak English secured a job and slowly moved up the ladder! It was incredibly difficult. Despite all the challenges, Mum was happy to take whatever job was available, for our sakes. She was able to get her first job at Bagel Time, where she worked the line making the minimum wage of $5.85 per hour. She often worked long hours plus overtime on weekends to earn more. Like language barriers, trouble with transportation was always an issue that challenged her. She took public transportation to and from work. Just as in Egypt, she got lost a couple of times because she got on the wrong bus. This was because she could not read the English signs and getting help was difficult due to the language barrier. To help with this issue, we wrote down our apartment address and phone number and asked her to keep it in her purse. This was the best we could do since the family did not own a car at the time and this helped her a lot.

As we began adjusting to our new life, America came under attack by Islamic terrorists on September 11, 2001. We witnessed one of the most painful moments in American history just six months after we arrived. The terrorists hijacked four airplanes, crashing two into the World Trade Center in New York City and another into the Pentagon in Arlington, Virginia. A fourth airplane crashed into the ground near Shanksville, Pennsylvania, as courageous passengers and crew fought for control from the hijackers. According to CNN news reports, more than 2,977 Americans lost their lives that day, and 6,000 people were injured (CNN 2019). I watched this horrific incident unfold on the TV in my ESL classroom. My ESL teacher, Mr. Franceschini, was from New York, and I could see the pain in his eyes as we watched those TV images of the twin towers crumbling and the Pentagon building burning.

My siblings and I are part of the American generation that vividly remembers the 9/11 attacks on US soil. I was twelve years old and in the sixth grade at Eastway Middle School. I remember that a brief announcement was made from the main office to inform students, teachers, and staff about the incident that was unfolding. The mood at school was different that day, as was the dismissal. Students milled around the hallways before slowly making their way outside. (Usually teachers stayed in their rooms working as students departed.) That day, teachers were in the halls or outside telling students to get to their respective buses to get home as quickly as possible. We were dismissed early from school. When my brother and I arrived home, we could see the sad faces of our parents. It was an unbelievable moment and heartbreaking to our parents as well. It was a sad day as an American, and I will never forget it, especially having only recently arrived in this country that gave our family the best it can offer. This day would profoundly influence my desire to later join the military and serve my new country. We grieved with our fellow Americans through this dark day and stayed resilient.

Towards the end of 2001, our family received our first car in America. It was a 1988 Buick Park Avenue with four doors, donated to the family through Catholic Social Services. The car was used yet in good condition and met our family's transportation needs. This was such a big day for us and a big blessing. Our family had never owned a car before, and we were grateful to receive such an amazing gift. The fact that my stepfather was disabled and often had to travel to the hospital gave my family priority over other families on the list to receive the car. Unfortunately, neither of my parents had a driver's license to operate this vehicle, so another South Sudanese refugee by the name of Giir Majok volunteered to drive us initially, which helped our family tremendously. My mother paid for all related fees, such as title, registration, license plate, and monthly insurance. My brother, whose English was limited, began the process of studying for a driver's license.

Our mother experienced discrimination and was bullied at her workplace because she was an African woman. At one point, she reported to my older brother that her coworker made fun of her because she had traditional tribal marks on her cheeks. Again, just as we had trouble with speaking English and transportation, we experienced cultural barriers in every aspect of our lives in our new country. Both my mother at work and we children at school had similar struggles adapting and being accepted—bullying and discrimination were experienced by all.

Our first apartment was affordable because my brother and my mother were able to work and pay the bills, but it was not really safe.

At school, black kids pushed us around. At home, it was our black neighbors who caused us the most anxiety. Dozens of eggs were smashed at our front door, and basketballs were bounced against the door to disturb our peace. To address this issue, my brother called 911 on multiple occasions, and the police were able to stop the disturbances, temporarily at least.

We feared for our lives at our first apartment, so we moved to a new place with the assistance of our Catholic Charities case coordinator. Our second home was a three-bedroom house at 2217 Eastway Drive, which used to be the Refugee Resettlement Office before they moved to uptown Charlotte. This home was perfect for our family. It allowed us to enjoy our peace quietly away from the noisy environment that we were thrown into during our first year in America. We had a large parking area to ourselves where we rode our bicycles donated by Martha, a woman who worked for St. John's Baptist Church. There was also a large green space to play soccer and football. We enjoyed the basketball hoop where we played pickup basketball with a few friends. We loved our new home!

In 2002, we experienced our first snowfall in America. For most of our neighbors, we learned snow was a familiar, if not frequent, experience. For newly arrived refugees from Africa, white snow represented something totally unprecedented. My siblings and I were intrigued by it, but we weren't afraid to go out.

On our TV screen, we saw kids our age outside in the snow having fun and building snowmen. We rushed outside at the speed of light to have a snowball fight. We got as creative as we could outside in the cold. We lay out in it and made some snow angels together—totally free fun for all! But while the snow was definitely a magical experience for us, we all got sick with colds after all the fun was over after that first snowfall.

When it snows in Charlotte, kids do not go to school, so they all love snow days. In 2002, Charlotte received more than two feet of snow! Our parents, who were not familiar with snowstorms, worried about power outages that could last for days and having enough food for us. We were not used to this type of weather, and it took us by surprise. For our family who knew warm weather, our first snowfall was a remarkable experience and a challenge at the same time. Whether we liked it or not, we had to adapt to the new weather in our new country.

My mother had accomplished so much in the short time since we arrived in America. Like any other woman who is the breadwinner of her family, my mother dreamed of not just putting a roof over our heads but also owning her own home. In 2003, she put in her application for a home with Habitat for Humanity. The application process consisted of application forms, a credit check, a personal interview, hours of volunteer work, and a current-home interview. She had an acceptable credit history, which included a good record of paying rent and utilities on time. She had about three years of stable income and employment history. She was able to demonstrate the ability to afford anticipated mortgage payments, including property taxes and homeowner insurance. By then, Mum had paid off the loan to the International Organization for Migration (IOM) and the US government for the plane tickets that brought my family to the US in 2001. This helped her establish her own credit and demonstrated that she was a good citizen.

Homeownership is a defining moment for all Americans. It demonstrates the ability of the individual to achieve success and prosperity through hard work and determination and is a key component of achieving the American dream. My mother's Habitat application was approved, and the work of building her home was begun. She was so excited about the news! My older siblings were the first volunteers, and they were fired up to build our house. They joined several volunteers and former homeowners to start the construction. My siblings Amal and Maywal took pride in the work. They took the responsibility and helped built our first house in America from the ground up and with joy in their hearts. By August 15, 2004, the family was happy to move into our new home near the Panthers Stadium in uptown Charlotte. It was an incredible experience and a great accomplishment. My mother's dream to own a house for her family came true. She now owned a five-bedroom, three-bathroom home, and the house was projected to be paid off by 2020.

In 2008, my mother was able to own two cars to support our family's transportation needs. One car she used to conduct family business, and the other was given to us to drive to school. When my mother was in Africa, the dream of owning her own car seemed impossible because of the circumstances and culture. Most of our transportation there was on foot from point A to B, and if we had money, we took the bus that was generally crowded. In Sudan, the majority of the population that owned cars were the Arabs. The Sudanese Arabs had the economic means to own nice houses, businesses, and companies, and held government positions. Sudan's Islamic regime discriminated against the black population. The Arab Sudanese had so many privileges to access all the country's resources, but the black African Sudanese had no upward mobility in a society that was ruled by sharia law. In the United States, however, opportunities were available, and the government assisted its citizens to become self-sufficient and self-reliant through social service agencies.

The fact that our mother was never allowed to go to school as ayoung girl has always bothered her. She had always highly valued education, not only for her children but also for herself. Coming to America gave my mother the opportunity to go to school and learn as she had once wished as a child. In 2012, she enrolled at Central Piedmont Community College (CPCC) while continuing to work to provide for the family. She was very dedicated to going to school as an adult and never missed a day. Her teachers noticed her desire to learn, and they were astonished by her passion once they discovered the fact that she was once denied an education in her home country. The chance to go to school, something that she always longed for, gave my mother closure. We children helped her with her homework and with English. When we were not around, it was her American-born grandson, Deng, who helped his grandma with assignments.

Looking back decades later, the most significant event in my mother's life has been the opportunity to bring her children and ill husband to the United States of America. In the midst of strife, upset, and unpredictability, my mother envisioned her family living in a place where peace, justice, equality, and prosperity were at the core of the national promise. America has fulfilled my mother's promise and hope for a better future. This is the country where my mother first learned to write her name and learned how to drive a car. Above all, America is the country where her children have had the opportunities she never did.

From left to right: Bol, Maywal, Amoe, Makot, Amal, and our mother in Charlotte enjoying our first snow. *Photo courtesy of Maywal Maywal.*

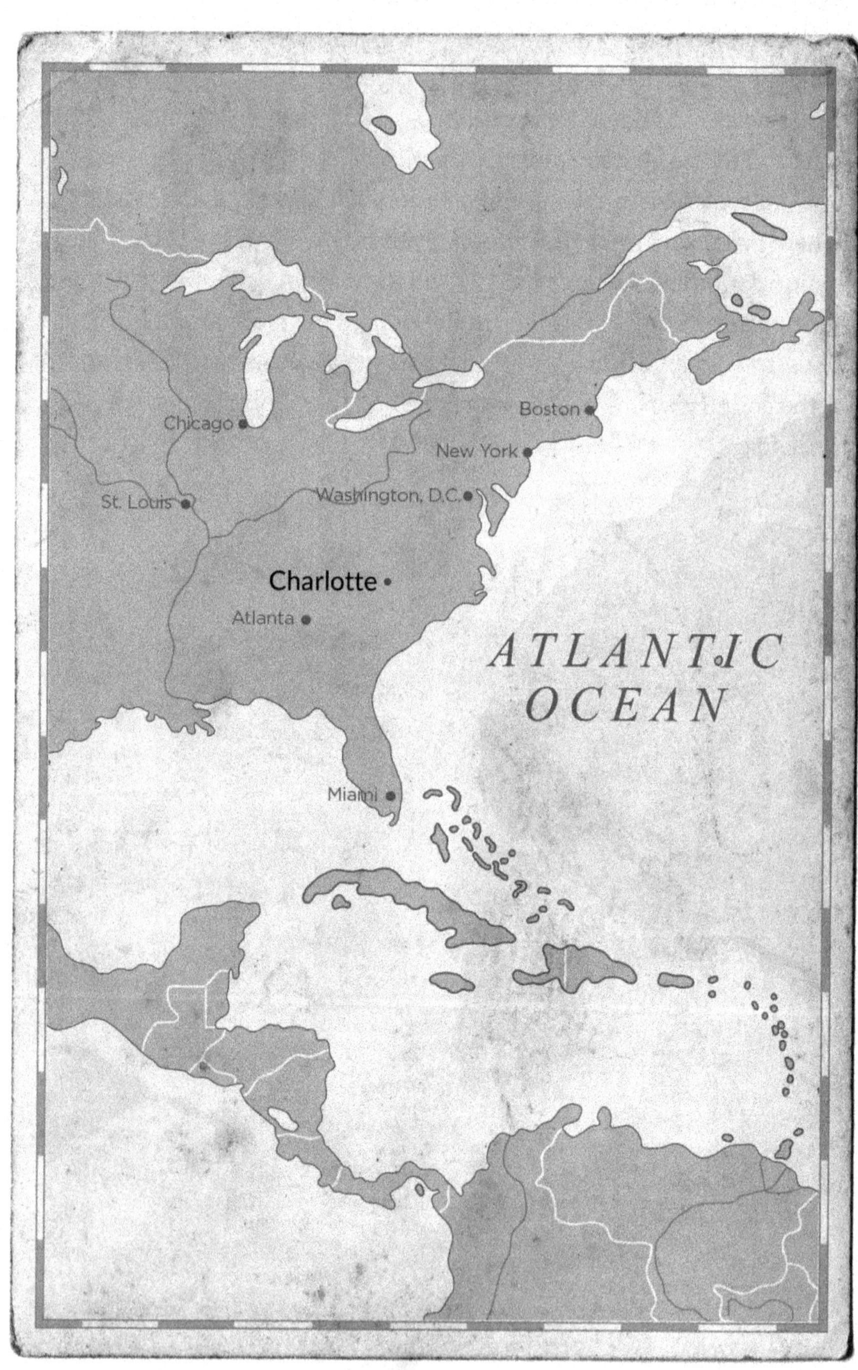

Chicago
Boston
New York
Washington, D.C.
St. Louis
Charlotte
Atlanta
Miami
ATLANTIC OCEAN

CHAPTER 6

Teenage Boys in America

**Children are the anchors
of a mother's life.**

– Sophocles, *Fragment 685, Phaedra*

My mother is the core of the family unit; she holds the family together through all difficulties, both in Africa and in the United States. She instilled in us values her parents instilled in her. At a young age, she taught us values such as respect, kindness, honesty, loyalty, fairness, compassion, and a strong work ethic. She emphasized a strong work ethic often because she wanted all her children to be responsible and independent in life. Growing up as a first-generation American in Charlotte, North Carolina, was a privilege compared to the village where my parents grew up.

Ten years after we arrived in the United States, most of my family members have become proud citizens of this great country. My stepfather, James Nagan, was one of the first in our family to take the test and become an American citizen. What does it mean to be an American? It means giving up loyalty to our former country and answering the call to sacrifice on behalf of America when called upon to serve in the military. In short, all it takes to be American is the will to become an American and the desire to contribute to the society in our unique ways. Being an American means accepting the diversity that is central to American culture, whether we like the melting pot or mixed-salad metaphor. What makes America the greatest country on the face of the Earth is not uniformity, but rather the assortment of heritages, cultures, and people who came before us to build this great nation. It was easy for us as children to adjust to the American culture. We became Americanized quickly and picked up on the language.

Sudanese culture is patriarchal. While Mum was (and still is) the core of the family, my stepfather, James, was the head of the family. He gave orders to all of us, including my mother. My stepfather controlled everything from the type of clothes we wore to the friends we kept. We had to request permission to step outside just to play football amongst ourselves or with friends. The chain of command in our family was crystal clear. It was my stepfather at the top, followed by Mum, and then my oldest brother. James was very strict, and everybody obeyed him without reservation, including Mum. He was a typical Sudanese man who accepted the male-dominated power offered to him by traditional patriarchal Sudanese society. Physically, he was a thin man of average height with smooth, dark skin. He was handsome and had an education level that was equivalent to high school. He spoke Arabic, Dinka, and Luo dialects fluently. He was an intelligent, confident, ambitious, and responsible man by all accounts. He is the biological father of two of my siblings, Amoe and Makot. I must admit that he took his fatherly duties seriously and helped my mother raise us all.

My stepfather and my mother had two distinctly different styles. Unlike my strict stepfather, my mother was kind and flexible with us. Where he was short-tempered, Mum was very patient, not only with us but also with him. My mother taught us from an early age to be obedient to James, and she also was obedient to him. She was brought up in a society in which men have power over women. Therefore, she never questioned decisions my stepfather made in the family, at least not in front of us.

My mother was naturally smart. She was a little older than my stepfather and much wiser than him, to state the truth. When we did something wrong, Mum preferred to speak to us about the issue instead of rushing to grab a belt to discipline us. Mum worked to pay the bills, and my stepfather handled issues of the house. Since he was the one who stayed home with us, he did not tolerate any nonsense from us. He kept us in line even though he was disabled. He did not really have the energy to spank us because he would get tired and become short of breath in the process.

James was a very stubborn man, and he was frank when he communicated his intention. He completely lacked tact and diplomacy. On the other hand, Mum was passive and more diplomatic with us. Her diplomatic skills lead to more successful outcomes and less difficulty or stressful communications. When I was a boy, my stepfather and I did not get along. As a result, I was spanked more often than any of my siblings. Most of that was due to my own stubbornness and my brave nature of questioning certain things I did not like.

When I reached my teenage years, I changed dramatically because of his fragile health. Whenever he was admitted to the hospital, he preferred me staying at the hospital with him over my other siblings. He began to notice my courage, and our relationship shifted for the better in my teenage years. We were not friends, but we understood each other very well. I had found an ally in my mother since I was a young boy. My stepfather never really established the father-son relationship with any of us. The only person who was close to him was my younger brother Makot. Growing up, we never called him "Daddy," nor did his biological sons. Our relationship was never strong, but he was indeed a father figure.

My siblings and I were raised in a stable family environment for the majority of our time in America. Like most families, ours was not immune to family issues. My brother Allah-jabo, who arrived in the United States as a teen, had fully grown up to be a man. Like my stepfather, Allah-jabo had authoritarian tendencies, and his personality always put him at odds with our family structure where James was the head. Allah-jabo and my stepfather could not get along when it came to family matters. To make the situation worse, both men lived under the same roof and ate at the same table. The disagreements and arguments between the two never ended peacefully. It got physical sometimes, and the family was often left on the verge of splitting. At one point, my stepfather called the police, and we saw our older brother handcuffed and taken way. My siblings and I were often left confused. A power struggle between these two men almost destroyed the family on several occasions. When the family was at the verge of collapse, it was my mother who had the courage and wisdom to keep it together.

It was never easy for Mum because she never wanted to take sides. She knew if she supported Allah-jabo, then my stepfather would feel isolated. On the other hand, if she stood with James, then my brother would feel like he was being pushed away. My stepfather did not want Allah-jabo to live with the family, and my brother wanted our stepfather to move out of the house. My stepfather felt Allah-jabo was a threat to his authority. On the other hand, my brother argued that my stepfather was taking advantage of Mum because she was not educated. There was merit to both arguments. My parents had joint bank accounts for the family. Whenever Mum received her paycheck, she gave it to my stepfather to deposit. The other source of income came from my stepfather's disability check. At the end of the month when bills were due, the family was always short financially. Later on, my mother discovered that my stepfather had drawn money from the account to send overseas to his relatives without her knowledge. The bank statement served as proof of what my stepfather had been doing. Mum did not have a problem with the help he provided to his relatives, but she took issue that my stepfather was dishonest in not telling her.

My stepfather was not a perfect man. Personally, I admired his courage and gave him the respect he deserved. After his surgery in 2001, he was declared disabled by the doctor. After that, he was always on life support. He had a large, stationary oxygen concentrator that he used to help him breathe and a smaller oxygen tank that he used outside the house. Despite his restrictions, my stepfather tried to help the family to the best of his ability. He drove Mum to and from work. When we overslept and missed the school bus, he drove us to school. Technically, he was not supposed to do any type of work that demanded physical strength, but he took it upon himself to help whenever he could. When our family needed food from the grocery store, my stepfather dragged his oxygen tank along and got in the car with me or one of my siblings to go food shopping. He always kept an extra oxygen tank in the car in case he ran low on oxygen while he was on the road. By 2007, my mother was able to get her driver's permit, and she eventually succeeded in driving herself to and from work. She hoped to free my stepfather from driving but could not convince him to stop completely.

In 2009, my stepfather's heath became extremely fragile, and he spent a lot of time in and out of the hospital. On one occasion, he had been in the hospital for three days, and on the fourth day, the doctor decided to do heart surgery. My mother arrived from work the day of the operation. I had been with my stepfather for the last two days. While we sat in the waiting room, my mother fell asleep, and I fell asleep about an hour later. Both of us were extremely exhausted. I remember feeling a strong breath of air rushing toward my body that forced me to suddenly wake up. My mother woke at the same time. The wind that I felt that day was my stepfather's spirit telling us goodbye. I have never in my life felt such an experience before. I knew my stepfather was already dead. We saw a nurse walk up to the reception desk and ask for Mr. Nagan's family. When we followed the nurse and met the doctor, we were told he did not make it. During the surgical procedure, the largest artery that is connected to the heart's left ventricle was accidentally cut. As a result, it caused bleeding that the doctors were not able to stop. He died at the Presbyterian Medical Center on June 15, 2009. He was only forty-four years old.

One of the challenges that came to my mother after my stepfather passed was raising teenage boys alone in America. The circumstances forced her, once again, to be a father and a mother. Like many other immigrant parents in the US raising children away from their homeland and extended family, she had a very daunting and challenging task. The reasons are enormous, including the culture of the society, which gives power and unlimited freedom to the children. Mum knew that our teenage years were crucial because it was a phase in our lives where we hovered between boyhood and manhood. My brothers and I fought each other several times. It was Amoe versus me, Maywal versus Amoe, Makot versus Amoe, and even my elder brother Allah-jabo got dragged into the boxing ring. It was crazy to have five boys all under one roof trying to prove their manhood and assert their power in a house where my mother was the only female as well as only parent. My mother dodged punches on several incidents when she attempted to break up a fight. She was courageous enough to make it crystal clear to all of us that her rules were supreme, and anybody who did not adhere to them would have to find his own family.

The experience of raising boys was certainly new to Mum because when she had four girls, her life was more peaceful. She once praised her daughters and described them as well-behaved children and easier to raise. We boys made her life more difficult because we were not easily manageable. When she first had my sisters, Mum was a quiet, young woman who did not find it necessary to scream while communicating with them. This was not the case with us. She learned to talk and learned to scream from the top of her lungs with her sons. With my sisters, she did not have to cook because my elder sister did most of the cooking. But with us, Mum had to cook much more food to make sure there was enough for growing teenage boys. In America, Mum's refrigerator and pantry needed to be fully stocked because she needed enough food to feed her five boys on any given day. On several occasions, Mum had to remind us to keep our clothes clean, our rooms clean, and ourselves clean. When we did all three, she was happy and encouraged us to keep up the good work. But when we did not, she was upset with us. However, through all the difficulties she never gave up on us, not even for a minute.

Mum's biggest worry about us was that we would choose street life and end up behind bars. Our house was not too far from the hood where it seemed drug dealers were around every corner. My mother was well aware of the problems that her sons could possibly face as teenagers. She did her best to prepare us to avoid these issues. In the US, drug abuse is a huge problem that affects millions of teenagers. My mother warned all of us about the dangers of drug and alcohol use. She constantly reminded us to be wise about those we picked to be our friends. "You are judged by the company you keep," she would often warn us. She once told us that alcoholic people have no future and drug usage has serious consequences that can affect the body and the brain.

In the fall of 2009, my brother Maywal, who was then twenty years old and a high school graduate, left North Carolina for Nebraska in an attempt to further his education. Sadly, that never happened. Despite the fact that Mum warned him not to go far, he did not listen. His help was needed in the family, and he could have continued his education in North Carolina. He left thinking he was making the right decision and was unaware that he was heading toward trouble. Midwest states have the highest Sudanese refugee population in the United States, and many of those refugees have turned to hip-hop and gang culture. The gang violence afflicting Sudanese refugees increased from weekend fist fights to drive-by shootings and robberies. Young South Sudanese were often victims and victimizers; some ended up in hospital beds, others behind bars, or killed.

Maywal might have used education as an excuse to leave North Carolina because he thought the Midwest would be an interesting place to live and enjoy party life. But his calculation was dead wrong! Nebraska was the hub for the Sudanese gangs that spread throughout Midwest cities. Omaha gave birth to gang groups such as South Sudan Soldiers, TripSet, and 402, who chose their name from the Nebraska area code. It was in Nebraska where my brother took the wrong path. He got pulled into the negative environment and hung around with the wrong crowd. Thank God he was not a member of any gang, but he followed kids who were convinced that their life's calling was to be rappers, and hip-pop culture was their way to achieve their goals. He started to party hard—drinking heavily, smoking weed, and chasing women. The idea of pursuing his education was watered down, and fun took priority. We had trouble communicating with him while he was in Nebraska because he avoided us.

Life became harder there for him, and instead of coming back home to North Carolina, he decided to move to Iowa. He fathered twins with a Sudanese girl he had met. The girl's parents were not happy, and they demanded that they speak to our mother. In the Sudanese culture, getting a girl pregnant without proper marriage comes with serious consequences. The girl's parents demanded compensation for the damage done to their young daughter. My mother sent our eldest brother, Allah-jabo, to Iowa to meet with the girl's parents and uncles. Allah-jabo, representing our family, took the message of apologies on behalf of our mother to the girl's family. Allah-jabo brought a cash dowry to the girl's family, and both families agreed that the girl, Suez, would join our family. Suez then came to North Carolina and was warmly accepted into the family. Maywal remained in Iowa. Things were done according to the southern Sudanese culture.

While the girl resided with the family, my mother wanted her to return to school once the twins were born. In the meantime, my mother took the chance to teach her basic things about motherhood. Suez was only seventeen and had no experience with raising children, but my Mum was committed to helping her succeed when she gave birth. Finally, Maywal returned to North Carolina, and the twins were born in 2010. He, Suez, and the twins left that following year for Des

Moines, Iowa. While in Iowa, the couple went their separate ways. Maywal went to Kansas City, Missouri, to reside there while Suez remained in Iowa with the kids and her family.

In spring of 2012, I received a message via Facebook from Suez's sister, Sarah, who told me, "Your brother got hit by a car." I quickly called her to learn how it happened. Maywal, who had been drinking and looking to buy weed, was hanging out with some of his friends in downtown when the car hit him. The driver was drunk as well. Maywal did not know how he got to the hospital, but he had been admitted for three days by then. He was severely injured but did not want Mum to know. I shared the information with my eldest brother, Allah-jabo. We did not want to tell Mum for fear that she might have a heart attack upon hearing that her son was almost killed.

Finally, Allah-jabo shared the news with Mum who was heartbroken and worried by this news. She said, "I could never imagine that he would turn to the street where something that terrible can happen to him and not bother to let me know," as tears dropped from her eyes. She picked up the phone to call him multiple times, but there was no answer on his end. For him to not answer her phone calls did not make the situation any better. Three weeks later, Maywal called Mum after he was released from the hospital. "How are you feeling?" my mother asked him. "I am doing well, Mum," he responded. When Mum asked about the incident, he said he was recovering, but he denied the fact that he was drunk when the incident occurred. My mother told him that he needed to come home to North Carolina after he fully recovered. He said he would after he gathered his compensation. Two years passed, and Maywal never returned as he promised. He had let down his mother and felt ashamed of himself.

I was a decent kid growing up in America as a teenager, thanks to my mother's words and wisdom. I never tried cigarettes, weed, alcohol, or drugs during my teenage years. These things were distant concepts marked with a big, fat, red X in my mind. I feel unique in the sense that I was the only kid among my peers and siblings who has never tried anything. Drugs and alcohol are a very big part of teen culture in America. I was simply not curious enough to try them. I had a different mindset as a teen. Even at that age, I looked at myself as a leader and a man of integrity. Therefore, I did not follow the wrong crowd like my brothers and friends did. Three out of my four brothers did drink alcohol in irresponsible ways and tried smoking weed at some point. Despite Mum's warnings, two of my siblings tried things out of rebellion, peer pressure, and sheer fun. Throughout my teenage years, I knew people who regularly smoked weed, sniffed cocaine, and got wasted drinking. While I disapproved, I think no less of them for it. Looking back, I am proud of my teenage years. I made wise decisions and have always been a positive influence for young people in my community, and they see me as a cool role model. For Mum, who had daughters before the sons arrived, it's fair to say that raising boys was much harder in America compared to the girls she raised in southern Sudan.

I can brag about my teenage years because I made it unscathed. As a teenager, I understood my mother's expectations of us, and I completely avoided all peer pressure. My unyielding discipline helped me meet her expectations. Valuable lessons learned through my own experience as a teen helped me make better decisions. First, I focused my attention on following through with Mum's expectations and aligning them with my own personal goals instead of the goals of my friends. Second, I knew I was a leader, and I did not like to follow others, and that helped me avoid the negative pressures. "Everyone's doing it" didn't pressure me. Third, I knew how to be my own best friend. Fourth, I knew my parents wanted the best for me and knew what that was, whereas my friends did not. Therefore, I listened to my mother, even though I was the most stubborn kid among my siblings.

From left to right: Maywal, Bol, and a mutual friend after graduating from Myers Park High School in 2008. *Photo courtesy of Allah-jabo Maywal.*

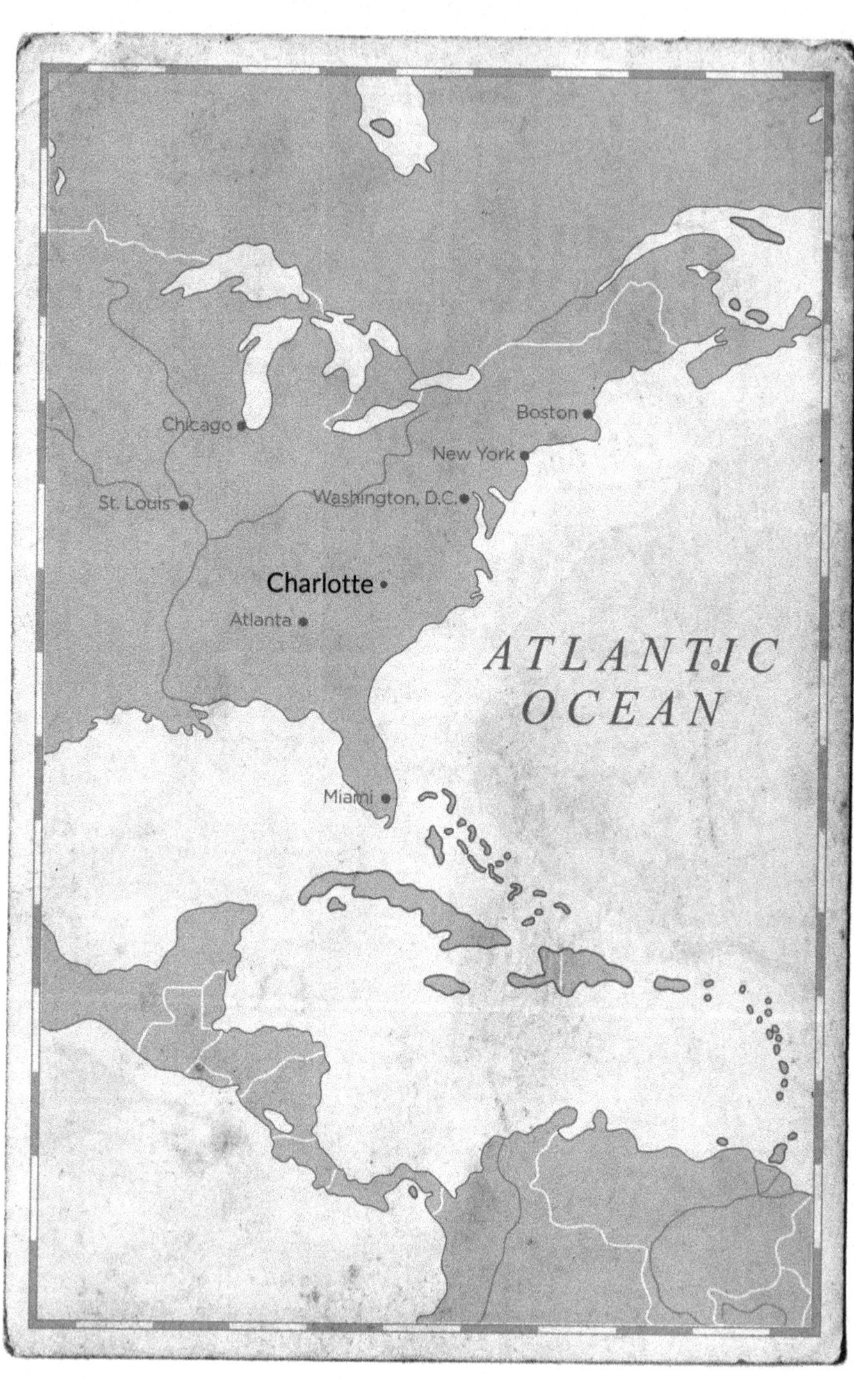

Chicago
Boston
New York
St. Louis
Washington, D.C.
Charlotte
Atlanta
Miami
ATLANTIC
OCEAN

CHAPTER 7

Entrepreneurial Heritage

**Start children off on the way they
should go,and even when they are
old they will not turn from it.**

– Proverbs 22:6 (NIV)

My mother's work ethic is incredible, and she instilled these values in us. We witnessed her hard work when we lived in extreme poverty in the displacement camps that arose from the flat, dusty plain in Sudan. The Jebel Aulia camp was home to thousands of southern Sudanese who fled their homes during the war. At Jebel Aulia, homes were squat mud-brick abodes with straw-thatched roofs; some had bright green or blue doors to contrast the pervasive brown mud buildings. In and around the area, a few skinny goats wandered freely; hungry dogs slept lazily in whatever shade they could find. The wind always blew, picking up sand from the ground. Plastic bags caught in the few weeds that sprang up. On the street, paper and empty food containers lay on the ground creating piles of trash. No jobs were available for the displaced people, and food was always scarce.

Despite the harsh conditions my family experienced, Mum always found a way to feed all of us. She did not depend on aid from the United Nations or World Food Programme (WFP). She bought coal and cooked over the fire. We ate one meal a day, and sometimes it was just okra stew with dry bread. When things got really tough, we ate only salted rice and drank plenty of water to top it off. When things were better, we ate baked beans with salt and meats such as fish or chicken—definitely a luxury because we could not afford it.

The source of our family income? Mum brewed alcohol from fermented dates, which were plentiful in Sudan. She learned the technique from her mother, who learned it from her mother, and so forth through countless generations. Fermented foods and beverages were native Sudanese traditions, just as they were for many ancient cultures all over the world.

After the Islamic regime took control of Sudan, brewing alcohol became illegal under sharia law, and anybody who brewed it was basically asking for trouble. While native Sudanese were diverse ethnically, religiously, and linguistically, few were Arab or Muslim. But the laws that governed the country came from the Quran and were strictly enforced on everyone, regardless of their religion.

Since we were conscious of the laws and the danger, our mother would brew alcohol late at night with the help of my older sister and would sell it in the morning. The dates were mixed with water and yeast and left to ferment for three days. Afterward the liquid was distilled, producing about eight liters of spirit-like alcohol per night. Once it was done, Mum sold about four to eight two-liter bottles a day. Brewing alcohol proved to be a highly lucrative way to make money after the sharia came into existence under then-President Jaafar Nimeiry. The majority of women who fled conflict in the south became "illegal" brewers to feed their families.

Some of Mum's customers were black Sudanese, but the majority were friendly Arab men who had no problem with poor, displaced people. Some were wealthy Arabs from Khartoum, and others were brick makers along the River Nile. The Arab customers would sneak out from their comfortable houses to come drink *marissa* or *araqi* ("alcohol" in Arabic) freely in the camp where their families or friends would not be able to judge them. The men would come and sit comfortably for a bit, accept some date wine, and chat before putting in their order. They drank heavily and, once they were satisfied, would hand over cash in Sudanese pounds for the araqi they purchased. Most were regular customers who would come about once a week with a large amount of money to blow on drinking.

On numerous occasions, police arrested those who were suspected of brewing alcohol. Once, police raided the displacement camp where we resided, arresting more than fifty-five women and burning down more than fifty shelters for allegedly brewing alcohol. My mother was almost caught with a half-gallon of araqi in her hand as the police were closing in on her. But thank God, she was able to hide it in the house. She had received the news a little late, or she would have buried it in our chicken room, which was unpleasant for police to search.

That day, the police came and conducted serious house-to-house searches, which can only be described as scary and dangerous. The families who had their shelters burned after the raid became homeless. The women who were arrested that day were thrown in a lorry that headed to prison. Those caught typically received 170 lashes in total, thirty days in detention with only one meal per day, and a fine of £250 Sudanese. The accused illegal brewers were sprayed with cold water on their bodies before they were pulled one by one to get their lashes. There was no justice or mercy for those women who were thrown in jail. The Islamic court that had jurisdiction over the native population never considered the faith of non-Muslims who held different beliefs. The laws were Islam, and it was one size fits all.

Before the police left the camp, the Arab officer who led the raid warned everyone about the serious consequences that came with brewing alcohol: "This is a Muslim country, and if you're caught drinking or your breath smells like alcohol, you will be arrested and lashed in jail. Am I clear?" The women in the camp were scared, but not by the officer's rhetoric. What scared them was the unexpected raid that took place and left several shelters destroyed. Typically, my mother and her colleagues knew that the police came about twice a week to check for alcohol because that was their routine, which allowed the brewers time to hide or bury their alcohol where it could not be found by the police. My mother had been brewing alcohol for more than sixteen years when she came so close to being caught. She said, "It's always possible to be caught, but knowing how to avoid being caught comes with experience."

Each night, when she was done brewing, she would pack up the three to four stills and bury the medium drums of alcohol outside the property. Mother's colleagues thought the reason she had never been caught was because she had magic that kept the police away from searching our house. This made my mother laugh. The reason she had never been caught was because she had dug strategic hiding places about five feet deep in different locations. They allowed her quick access to bury all the brewed alcohol within sixty seconds. In our small mud-walled home, she had dug up one area inside the chicken room where chickens were always pecking the dirt floor outside the house. The chicken room was a great spot because nobody would ever look at it.

My mother made it clear to all of us that the pain that comes with work can be endured and will not kill. If you want something, then you must work for it and not expect easy ways or handouts in our family. At an early age, my siblings and I were expected to work alongside our parents.

When we built our first mud house in the Jebel Aulia displacement camp, we all pitched in to build it from the bottom up. First, we dug up the reddish clay. Then we added water and made the clay into mud blocks using a wooden form. We left the mud blocks to dry in the sun for a day or two. When the blocks were ready, we started building by stacking the mud blocks with a mud-clay mortar. We had to secure materials such as zinc for the roof after the walls reached ten feet high. My cousin, brother, and I were tasked to go out and cut the supplies from the surrounding bush to erect bush poles and roofing straw. My mother and sisters had to collect water from a water pump. The average distance they had to travel was six kilometers (nearly four miles) on foot, and the weight of the water they carried on their heads was about twenty kilograms (forty-four pounds). Only by binding together as a single force were we able to build our own shelter under the heat of the African sun. Our shelter was not built through the UN "blue tent" program for refugees; it was built with our own hands and sweat. It was through this experience that we understood the value of work ethic.

My mother often reminded us that dreams and work go together. "If you have a dream that you want to achieve, trust your instinct and follow your heart," she would advise all of us. "Never rest until you sleep on it and protect it. You must show real dedication and persistence because that will determine whether you will achieve it or not."

My brother Allah-jabo showed Mum's strong work ethic since he was young. Back in the displacement camp in Sudan, he had his first job as a shoeshine boy. During the nineteenth century, shoeshine boys plied the trade on the streets, particularly in major cities like Kassala, Khartoum, Ad-Damazin, and Omdurman because these were the areas where professionals congregated. While they weren't all criminals, some moonlighted as pickpockets and shoplifters, so the police force in Khartoum spread negative images in order to crack down on the boys and round them up. In today's world, an increasingly enlightened attitude toward the shoeshine jobs has removed the old-fashioned hierarchical point of view. It's now considered a business, and some cities require shoeshiners to have a license to conduct their business legally.

But back then, no license was required to work legally, and kids like my brother had to be creative to attract customers. Allah-jabo was a very creative and talented teen with a winning personality and the ability to speak fluent Arabic. In his shoeshining box, he had twelve colors of polish, twelve brushes, six polish cloths, and other accessories that he needed. Unlike the majority of his peers, Allah-jabo offered extra services, such as shoe repairs and general watch repair. His ability to think outside of the box was what distinguished Allah-jabo from the rest of his peers. He understood that "necessity is the mother of invention," and he was very successful in conducting business at such a young age. His success as a shoe polisher, shoe repairman, and a watch repairman on the streets of Khartoum resulted in an incredible amount of profit that contributed to our family's financial stability. At age fifteen, my brother was already a successful entrepreneur with no prior business experience or training at all. With more than one occupation, Allah-jabo was bringing home £500 Sudanese after two weeks. This was money earned fairly through hard work and sweat and under the heat of the African sun in an unsafe environment.

Despite the fact that Allah-jabo was bringing money to assist the family, my parents did not approve for several reasons. First, they worried for his safety on the streets of Khartoum. Second, my parents knew that Allah-jabo was very intelligent since he exceled academically in school. Therefore, they did not want him to be chasing money at such a young age, especially when my mother and stepfather provided for the family. It was in the best interest of Allah-jabo to be in school and be a normal child like other children. When Allah-jabo came home from school, he would sneak out of the house without being noticed and go polish shoes on the streets of Khartoum. He would return around 10 p.m. and find my parents waiting for him by the door with a leather belt. He used to get spanked regularly for sneaking out of the house and pursuing an occupation that my parents did not approve of. When Allah-jabo would get spanked for sneaking out, he would promise my parents not to go out again. Ten minutes later, he would grapple a handheld kerosene lamp and stay up to study and do his homework. The majority of children from age twelve to seventeen who did shoe polishing were not likely to complete school because they would drop out. My parents knew Allah-jabo was a great kid, but they worried that this occupation would destroy their innocent son's future.

Shining shoes was undoubtedly an important source of income for many poor, displaced children and their families around displacement camps in Sudan. Since the war started between the government in Khartoum and the rebels, most of the displaced children lived in extreme poverty and were not afforded basic protections. Government forces and government-backed militias abducted these children as a form of recruitment. These children experienced rape and other human rights abuses. In the 1990s, the Human Rights Watch report *Sudan: "In the Name of God," Repression Continues in Northern Sudan* said that the Sudanese government in Khartoum rounded up hundreds of boys displaced by the war, the majority southern, in markets and on the streets of Khartoum and other cities (Human Rights Watch/Africa 1994). The boys were summarily dispatched to religious camps where they were beaten for small breaches of discipline and given an Islamic education and Muslim names in order to convert them by force to Islam, regardless of their or their families' beliefs. Their traditional names were replaced by Arab names. Boys as young as fifteen years old received religious indoctrination and were incorporated into the government militia.

Multiple times, Allah-jabo was arrested while conducting his shoeshine business and was often severely beaten and thrown in jail. He would escape whenever the opportunity presented itself and made it home with injuries. This type of abuse by Sudanese state security was what my parents worried about and why they told Allah-jabo to stop pursuing his shoeshine business. On several occasions, two to three months would go by without the family knowing his whereabouts. This was always a signal to my parents that Allah-jabo was in trouble, and they did whatever possible in their power to find him. In 1997, paramilitaries and armed groups aligned with the government forcibly recruited thousands of children, including Allah-jabo, and forcibly conscripted them into the government armed forces for military training. Allah-jabo played Sudanese Army for a while to fool the authorities and then escaped later. Pro-government militias, such as a the one led by General Paulino Matip and Dr. Riek Machar, were known to round up displaced children in their early teens to be personal bodyguards and to increase the militia's manpower to assist the regime's fight in southern Sudan. After being abducted by force, boys like my brother were given brief military training on equipment and military tactics and then deployed to southern Sudan to fight in combat against their will.

When we arrived in the United States in 2001, Allah-jabo had two passions: business and becoming a lightweight boxer. Since he was young enough to resume his education, my mother advised him to go to school. He refused because he wanted to pursue a career in boxing, but conditions in a new country forced him to take a different path. His first job was at the Knife Company where he made minimum wage. He held that job for a year, then started working at the Marriot Hotel in uptown Charlotte. At the hotel, he worked in the dish room, food service, and as a waiter. The hotel job did not pay well, but his professionalism and friendly smile earned him decent tips from guests. After working at the Marriot for a while, he found another job at the FedEx Shipping Center. This job paid well, but it was physically demanding and stressful. He humbly worked there for a while before he revisited his dream of wanting to be his own boss.

Allah-jabo knew that there was something bigger for him. So he decided to test his ambition in America, a country where opportunities are real and dreams can be achieved. In 2003, my brother returned to what he loved to do and what he was born to be: a businessman! He started off driving for one of the cab companies in Charlotte. As a taxi driver, he was working more than ninety hours a week driving through the city of Charlotte and other cities picking up customers and dropping them off. Driving a taxi was by far the best job he ever had because he worked on his own schedule, made money, and came home to watch Friday night fights on TV. Once he saved up enough money to start his own business, he got seriously ill. The dream of wanting to blaze a trail toward owning his own business one day was put on hold by circumstance.

In mid-2003, Allah-jabo was diagnosed with cancer. Cancer comes out of left field and throws you onto a battlefield, whether you are ready to fight or not. It came at him hyper-fast and left him stuck in a world of major life-or-death choices. As a former boxer and someone who coached boxing, Allah-jabo chose to fight. He had dreams, and cancer was not going to stop him. Figuratively, his old boxing gloves were dusted off, and he courageously prepared for a long fight against cancer.

The day of his surgery, my brave mother went to Presbyterian Medical Center at 4 a.m., three hours in advance, to comfort Allah-jabo before his operation and show he was not alone in the fight. One of Allah-jabo's good friends and I accompanied Mum. The surgery went well, and Allah-jabo was released three days later. His regular work schedule was interrupted with regular visits to the hospital and chemotherapy treatments. During the period of his treatment, he lost a lot of weight and his voice. The family was affected greatly by his illness. Communicating with him was difficult, and he had to write down everything he wanted to say. My stepfather was already out of work because of disability due to illness since Egypt. Before Allah-jabo became ill, it was he and my mother who were working and providing for the family. The family simply could not afford another person to be ill, especially in a new country.

Throughout the time Allah-jabo was ill, my mother always made special soup just for him. When she got home from work, Mum got in the kitchen to fix hot chicken soup and brought it to him. At that time, Allah-jabo did not reside with our family, so she had to use public transportation to take whatever she had cooked to him. The family did own a car at the time, but my mother did not know how to drive yet. My mother always prayed for Allah-jabo to recover quickly and get back up. I heard my mother pray for him once, and it was powerful! I cannot describe how powerful her words were because I was so moved by them and her soul.

During the time my brother was sick, I temporarily lived with him at his apartment on Morningside, and I saw him feed himself through a tube. I offered to assist, but he refused and confidently told me, "Bol, I got it little brother! Don't worry." I saw him lift himself out of the bed and get up to walk to the restroom and then to the kitchen. Slowly but surely, he was moving on his feet and started to join me in the living room more often to watch TV. One night, he joined me to watch *Sports Center*, and he asked me for the remote controller. I gave it to him, and he switched the channel to HBO, and I quickly realized there was an important fight that night that he did not want to miss! As a former boxer, my brother lived by the motto "never give up and never give in," and that boxing mindset helped him stay positive in the face of obstacles in life. Once he was on his feet, he started to "throw punches" at cancer, and slowly his health began to improve. I was amazed by his fighting spirit!

As months slowly rolled by, my brother kept pounding cancer day in and day out through faith in God, mental toughness, and being an active participant in the battle with a positive mindset. At the beginning, when he received the diagnosis, he was depressed and terrified and felt helpless. After months of battling cancer, his health significantly improved. With the help of the family, he became more confident. In 2004, my brother gained back all the weight he once lost, and his voice slowly came back. He was eating normally again and slowly recovered like a champion.

After he recovered, his mounting medical bills awaited him, and that meant he had to hustle to pay them off. One thing I noticed about my brother was resilience. No matter what problems life threw at him, no matter how deep the hole he found himself in, he always found a way to bounce back and overcome adversity. That's the mentality of a boxer, and that's my brother!

He returned to driving again and worked a few hours until
his health fully stabilized. By 2005, my brother started his own
transportation business with only one Lincoln Town Car, and gradually
he added several more. As the number of his vehicles increased, he
hired drivers to come and work for him. Even though he hired drivers,
he never sat back and waited for the phone to ring. He was out on the
street driving and constantly trying to move his business forward. His
winning personality allowed him to win a two-year contract for a strip
club in uptown Charlotte.

By 2007, my brother's private transportation business was thriving,
just like it did when he was a young shoeshine boy on the streets of
Khartoum, Sudan. He understood that ambition and hustle are the
keys to success in business. My brother had achieved so much within
a short amount of time, but the sky was the limit, and he wanted
to aim high in order to see the full potential of his dream. He once
told me, "I discovered a long time ago as a teen that self-limitation
voices that come through our heads with regard to risk in business
are false. There is no limit to the human ability to adapt or the human
imagination to invent the future that creates opportunities. You must
dare to invent the future." That night, I realized my brother's ambition
and hustle had not changed at all since he was young. He was still
that stubborn and ambitious kid that got spanked a lot when he used
to sneak out of the house to go polish shoes.

At age twenty-five, Allah-jabo was his own boss and someone
who truly believed that the ultimate responsibility for his life and
limitations began and ended with himself. Without a question in his
mind, he was the master of his own fate. Deep down in his heart,
he also knew his success in business was a victory for our family.
Therefore, he pressed on to invent an even greater future for our
family because he knew how far we had come.

Toward the end of 2007, he kept one town car as his personal
vehicle and turned the other vehicles into taxis. He went on to buy
more vehicles to eventually get to thirty vehicles that were needed
for him to start his taxi company. For most taxi businesses, the single

greatest startup challenge is the expense of purchasing vehicles. However, he was able to manage it on his own. Shortly after he secured the number of vehicles required by the city, he installed several pieces of equipment, such as taxicab meters, radios, GPS, and top lights for his taxis to help riders easily identify the cabs. He did the majority of the work on his own to save money. By week two, all his new cars were insured, professionally painted, and decals and logos attached. His cab company was rolling on the streets of the Queen City competing with other big companies. He named his taxi company Professional Cab.

It was a great achievement, not just for my brother but also for the Maywal family as a whole. My mother was happy and proud of Allah-jabo. She liked to see him succeed and do well in business. "Hard work is going after the things you want. You have to be bold and dedicated enough to put in the work that gets you there," Mum would remind us once again. In addition to his cab company, Allah-jabo added two limousines and party buses to diversify his business. His business was gradually moving forward and doing well compared to other small transportation businesses in the city.

The first two years were great, and then the clock began to turn on him as years passed by. Despite the success, his business hit stumbling blocks that pushed him into debt for a year. He worked hard and pulled himself out of debt. When 2008 rolled around, his taxi company was dragged into the financial crisis known as the Great Recession. Economically, he struggled month by month to pay his expenses and the drivers who worked for him. Despite the challenges, he remained positive and continued to hustle hard in order to stay in business. By June 2009, the US recession eased, and my brother's business was able to make ends meet once again.

In 2014, my brother's taxi company, along with other cab companies, was blocked from doing business at Charlotte Douglas International Airport. The only cab company that did business at the airport was Yellow Cab, whose owner allegedly bribed Charlotte Mayor Patrick Cannon to pass a law designating the Yellow Cab

Company as the official airport vendor. The airport was the center of gravity for taxi businesses because it was open 24/7/365. When small taxi companies like my brother's got pushed out of the airport, it hurt all those that were playing by the rules to compete.

On March 26, 2014, the mayor was arrested on charges of accepting over $48,000 in bribes from undercover FBI agents who posed as businessmen willing to work with the city (CBS News 2014). In addition to choosing a replacement for the former mayor, Charlotte City Council reviewed policies that might provide opportunities for my brother and others. On April 4, 2014, my brother had the courage to appear on our local news channel WBTV to voice his concern regarding the unfair taxi policy at the airport (Crump 2014). He said, "The scandal involving the former Charlotte mayor raises the issue that the city council needs to revisit its codes for taxis and limos." With regard to corruption and politics, Charlotte council member Patsy Kinsey strongly felt the issue should go beyond the taxi industry. For someone like my brother to work hard, play by the rules, and buy new vehicles and credit card machines, and still get shut out of places like the airport was just unfair to him and other small businesses.

Unlike the majority of entrepreneurs, my brother never had a four-year degree in business administration. He started from scratch by pulling himself up by his own bootstraps to shape his own destiny. My brother's childhood strongly influenced his views on pursuing opportunity, but not in the way many people might expect. Allah-jabo was the toddler my mother tied on her back when she fled South Sudan in 1983. They spent weeks in the bush dodging bullets and avoiding wild animals before they made it to the displacement camp in northern Sudan. At age twelve, he began sneaking out of the displacement camp every day looking for that next opportunity to polish shoes and contribute to the family's financial stability.

When we arrived in the United States, he bounced around among different jobs until he returned to business and started his first successful transportation business. Starting a business is like moving a mountain by yourself; it's a challenging and stressful endeavor by its very nature. Achieving entrepreneurial success under difficult circumstances was a great accomplishment. Our mother instilled and demonstrated the value of work that can lead to achieving our dreams.

I know my brother as an entrepreneur who defied incredible personal odds, including war, serious illness, extreme poverty, discrimination, and even politics to raise above these obstacles and start his company. He has not yet achieved all his dreams, but he is a winner.

Left to Right: Makot Maywal, Amoe Maywal, Deng Maywal, Moses Goi, Bol Maywal, baby Piol, Adout Goi, Amal Maywal, Allah-jabo Maywal. Allah-jabo Maywal drove the family to Belmont Abbey College using one of his business-owned limousines as the family attended Bol's graduation in 2013.

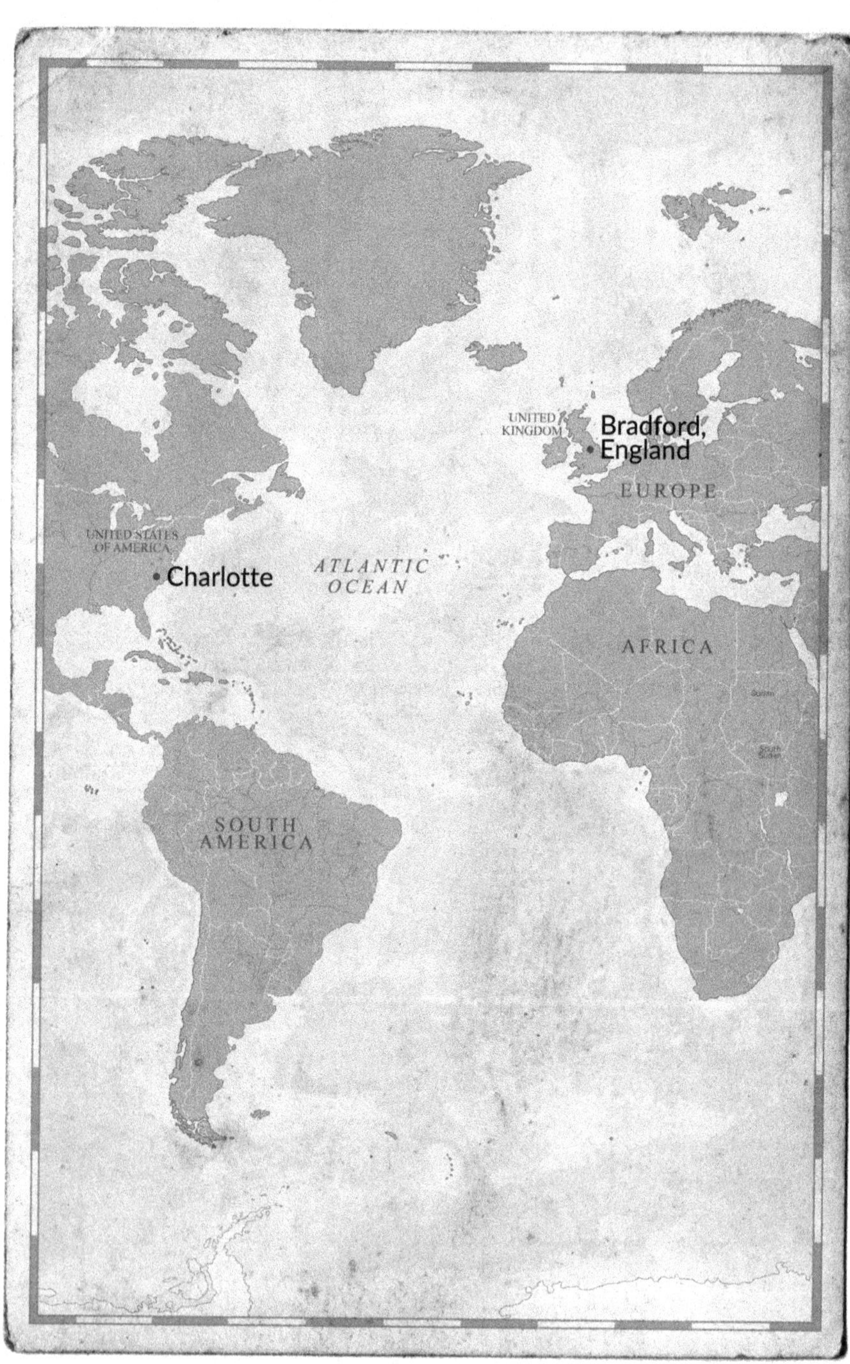

UNITED KINGDOM
Bradford, England
EUROPE
UNITED STATES OF AMERICA
Charlotte
ATLANTIC OCEAN
AFRICA
SOUTH AMERICA

Knowledge, Power & Peace

**Education is the most powerful weapon
we can use to change the world.**

– Nelson Mandela, address at the Planetarium,
Johannesburg, South Africa, July 16, 2003

When it came to education, my mother was our biggest cheerleader. As a young girl, she dreamed of becoming a doctor. She grew up in the village and received traditional African education. The learning she and her siblings received was oral instruction because the knowledge was stored in the heads of the elders.

Her first instructors were her parents, and they had the task of imparting knowledge, skill, and attitudes to prepare their children for success. The teaching was informal, didactic, and practical. It was done in the style of stories, legends, riddles, and sometimes songs. Her parents put emphasis on practical learning, and the children learned by watching, participating, and then executing what they learned. The skills included house management, cooking, carving, sewing, masonry, clay working, building, canoe making, building a mud hut, and making cloth from animal skins. These were the basic skills, knowledge, and attitudes that allowed individuals to live and function effectively in the community.

Her parents made sure that their children learned by doing. My grandma often told her children, "The best way to learn sewing is to sew; the best way to learn farming is to farm; the best way to learn cooking is to cook; the best way to learn how to fight is by wrestling." My grandparents passed these words down to their children, and then my mother passed them to us to teach us the importance of learning.

In my mother's generation, teaching was not limited only to parents. Other family members, experienced elders, and community leaders did their part educating the young. Learning was not separated from other spheres of community activity. It was the whole life of the community and had no special time of day or place. Mum shared that learning is a life-long process in which an individual acquires wisdom through skills, knowledge, and values from birth until death.

As my mother and her siblings became teenagers, they received more education in order to go through the rites of passage and to be considered adults. Boys and girls learned about their roles at home and in society. The finals days of the rites of passage required no paper, formal exams, or certificates, but the learners graduated ceremoniously. The learner was considered a graduate when they were able to show that they were brave enough to be considered a young man or woman. Most girls her age were taught skills related to home management, midwifery, health care, weaving, and farming. Mum learned how to become a good mother and how to handle her husband soon after marriage. Males like her brothers were prepared to become warriors, manual farmers, good fathers, and other male-dominated occupations such as fishing. A ceremony was held for my mother when she reached age fifteen to mark completion of the traditional rites of passage and education from her parents and community elders. The traditional African education that my mother received was functional because the knowledge, skills, and values taught were relevant to the socioeconomic activities of the individual in that society. This was evident in the fields of agriculture, building mud huts, carving, sewing, and child rearing. But she was not literate in the sense of the formally educated world.

Formal education for African indigenous people came with the influx of foreigners to Sudan. In the early 1950s, Sudan was a British colony. In northern Sudan, the education system was influenced by Egyptian Arabs and was therefore Islamic. Muslims and Christians both hoped to win the south. British missionaries were sent from Khartoum to southern Sudan to set up several missionary schools with the goal of producing new teachers and religious leaders to propagate Christianity among the indigenous population. The Christian missionaries also provided academic and vocational training, and strongly discouraged the traditional practices of the local people. The attempt to evangelize indigenous people took place at the same time as ruthless European and northern Sudanese Arab traders were savaging southern Sudan in their quest for ivory and slaves. The indigenous people rejected European and Arab attempts to change their way of life and how they educated their children. Therefore, the majority of indigenous people in the south, including my grandparents, adopted a negative attitude toward missionary schools and never allowed their children, including my mother, to attend school.

Despite the fact that most indigenous people rejected Westernization and Christianity, a few were successfully converted to Christianity. These small groups of locals did not have negative attitudes toward alternative education provided by the Christian missionaries. Therefore, they voluntarily sent their children to schools for education instead of out into the fields to herd goats. My mother's parents eventually did change their negative view somewhat about education that was provided by "foreigners" in southern Sudan, but they were not completely swayed. My grandparents allowed one of their children, my Uncle Chan, to attend school, and he was the first in our family to receive a formal education. He was the first to speak, read, and write a foreign language.

When Mum arrived in the US, her desire to go to school was strong. The fact that she was deprived of education as a young girl bothered her. Coming to America was an opportunity to revisit her long-cherished dream of wanting an education for herself. It was a personal goal, but it was certainly not easy with her work schedule, looking after us, and other commitments. At age fifty-five, my mother went to school for the first time in her life and enrolled at Central Piedmont Community College (CPCC) in uptown Charlotte. At the community college, she took English as a Second Language and basic math courses. Unlike older people who feared to return to school, Mum never feared that she was too old for school. She felt she needed to catch up and learn as much as she could. She is one of many who have tackled their fear and proven that people are never too old to return to school. Attending CPCC gave her a chance to interact with others and make friends. She enjoyed going to community college despite juggling other responsibilities. It gave her as sense of closure and made her feel happy.

While we were in Sudan, living in the displacement camp, my siblings and I attended a school that had no electricity, seats, food, or running water. We walked more than ten miles on foot to get to school and back. At school, we sat under a tree with empty stomachs. My siblings and I had a little education later in Egypt. During these difficult times, Mum never stopped being our biggest cheerleader. She always encouraged us to go to school despite the harsh conditions we were in.

After we arrived in America, my siblings and I began school at Crown Point Elementary in Charlotte without knowing English. In August 2001, I joined Maywal and Amal at Eastway Middle School. At Eastway, we were in an English as Second Language (ESL) classroom along with refugees from Somalia, Congo, Bosnia, Vietnam, and other countries. The ESL classroom was like a United Nations General Assembly because it was very diverse with students from different countries. From the start, we were all academically behind. The ESL teachers were great, and they cared about the future of the students they taught. It became obvious to our teachers that my siblings and I needed more help because we could neither read nor write English. They dedicated time to helping us learn how to read and write in English through one-on-one tutoring on subjects such as math, science, and US history. School was difficult for us since we were academically behind, but we were determined to learn. Our ESL teachers at the time helped us get caught up.

We also faced cultural challenges that made learning difficult. Above all, being bullied was the toughest challenge we faced at school. My siblings and I had the "fresh off the boat" look when we first entered our American school, and that made it hard to blend in among predominately (so-called) African Americans. It was obvious that we were new because we did not look like other kids, at least in the eyes of black students. This made us easy targets. We did not wear clothes and shoes that were popular or the latest brands. We simply wore whatever was donated to us by Catholic nuns who gave clothes and shoes to newly arrived refugees. We wore whatever fit. When our parents did have money, it did not go toward shoes and clothing. Instead, it would be used for utilities, food, and other essentials.

Nothing made school more difficult than being bullied by kids who looked like us, from our perspective. What do I mean by kids who looked like us? Well, our bullies were black kids! They were African Americans, our brothers and sisters with whom we share many things in common. It was something my siblings and I could not comprehend, and we were shocked by this horrible experience. We did not know that blacks did not like Africans until we attended Eastway. We were bullied by blacks for being dark skinned and African. One day while we were on the school bus, we got stuff thrown at us. We reported it to the bus driver, who was a black woman. She stopped the bus and went to the back to confront whoever had thrown things. Well, that did not help, and it went on several times during that ride until we reached school. At school, the bus driver attempted to have those kids written up (disciplined), but they disappeared and ran away.

Our ESL classroom was a very friendly environment where our teachers were supportive and classmates friendly. In other classrooms, however, we got bottles of water, soda, and chips thrown at us because we were different. We were called many names that were very offensive, including "African booty scratcher." There were times our bullies became physical, and we got hit or smacked on the backs of our heads. My siblings and I always walked away from the kids who pushed us. The same black kids with whom we shared our African ancestry were the ones who pushed us around in the hallway. We did our best to avoid these brothers and sisters of ours, but they would not stop their unacceptable behaviors. At times, we were forced to defend ourselves in situations where we were being harmed physically. They started fights that were often bloody for us. In self-defense, my brothers and I fought back, but we were often outnumbered and went home with bruises. Our parents were traumatized by these series of events. We were suspended from school from time to time for fighting, and being out of school for a week affected our academic performance.

In 2006, my brother Amoe, who attended Marie G. Davis Middle School, was found unconscious in the boys' bathroom. A black kid who had previously bullied him had snuck up on him and hit him on the back of the head, knocking him out completely. After the incident, an eye witness ran to the main office to report the situation. Someone, possibly school staff, poured water in his face to get him conscious. My parents received a phone call, and my stepfather, who could not speak English, went to school to pick him up. My stepfather was shocked by the incident. The school staff should have called an ambulance to take him to the hospital and get him checked, but that did not happen. A full investigation should have taken place to find that kid and punish him. Unfortunately, that did not happen because my brother was African. School staff should have done more, but they took advantage of my stepfather, a refugee who could not speak English. In this incident, my parents almost lost their child to bullying in an American school.

One day, I was at the cafeteria enjoying my lunch when I was approached by three black kids who previously bullied me. One of them was Jeremiah, the instigator and leader of the pack. His boys were standing around him like body guards. All of them had their arms folded. Jeremiah came and sat next to me and started to stare at me from my head to my toes as if he were doing some kind of inspection.

Then he said, "Wassup, bro!? What kind of shoes you got on?" I did not respond to him because I was eating my food and thought it best to ignore him. He continued, "Big dog, I said wassup, cuz? Where your J's at?!" I told him that I did not have to wear a pair of Air Jordans and that I was happy with what I had on. Then he said, "I know you got those shoes from Walmart, bro. What's the matter? You can't talk?" One of his boys jumped in and said, "Damn, nigga, your skinny ass is hungry, aren't you? I see why you ain't talking." I told him to get out of my face. As soon as they heard me talk, they all started to laugh out loud as if they had heard something funny.

At that point, I was still calm and able to control my temper. Then Jeremiah said, "This is America, and it's a black school, bro. Everybody wears Jordans and not some ugly ass shoes like what you got on. You need to learn how to dress like black folks do, man. And what kind of pants you got on anyway?" Finally, I finished eating and was ready to go. Jeremiah grabbed my shirt from behind and said, "Look, bro, we ain't gonna kick your ass today, but we'll get you another day. Anyway, why are you trying to look cool with them Walmart shoes? You ain't got some Jordans or a pair of Air Force 1s?"

I told him to get his hands off me. I made it clear to him and his buddies not to worry about what shoes or clothes I wore. As Jeremiah continued to talk trash about me, his buddies were laughing their lungs out. They laughed so hard and loud to the point they attracted other black kids to join them, as if there was some kind of show going on. I left as soon as I realized that more people were coming and the situation was getting worse.

Jeremiah and his buddies were not right about how they picked on me. I was aware of the popularity of Air Jordan shoes. But I didn't care

whether I wore Air Jordans or not! My siblings and I went to school
for an education.

When Michael Jordan's shoes first arrived on the shoe scene,
they were hugely popular. Many people wanted a pair, and there
were often riots and fighting over who would get the most popular
shoes on the planet. I'm certain Michael Jordan never anticipated
how popular these shoes would become when he ruled the court, but
each additional version of Jordan's signature shoe line is as popular as
the last one. Every year, a new Air Jordan shoe is unveiled, and each
one has been met with ever-increasing anticipation from the media,
the industry, and the buying public. At the heart of the product is the
perfect synergy between athlete and technology. Michael Jordan is
generally accepted as one of the greatest players in the history of
basketball, and the shoes he's worn throughout his illustrious career
epitomize his relentless dedication to performance, innovation,
and achievement.

The thing that Jeremiah and his friends did not know about
me was the fact that I knew of Michael Jordan and respected his
athleticism and legacy. If they had come to apologize to me about
how they mistreated me in the cafeteria, then I would have accepted
their apologies and even opened up to talk about my love for
basketball. I would not have minded playing a basketball game with
them and showing my skills since we all had gym together.

Shortly after we arrived in the US, I began to love basketball and
admired how Michael Jordan played the game. He changed the NBA
and was the leader of the basketball industry. Nobody would ever
take that away from Jordan. It's something he earned through his hard
work, determination, loyalty, and love of the game. If those kids who
bullied me had patience, they would have known that I was part of
the generation that was inspired by Jordan's greatness, but they had a
negative view of Africa and its people.

While I was at Eastway, I always wondered if they had any idea
how horrible it was to live as a refugee, walking barefoot from one
country to another, and all the other difficulties we faced. Would they

have changed their silly attitude about the shoes or clothes I wore? That day I was bullied by Jeremiah and his buddies in the cafeteria, I had on used, red and white Daxx men's lightweight lace-up running sneakers. Jeremiah had told me that Eastway was a black school and that blacks wore Jordan shoes along with another brand of Nike sneakers. Obviously, he did not know what it means to be black, nor was he familiar with what Jordan said about being black: "I realize that I am black, but I like to be viewed as a person, and this is everybody's wish." It was my wish also to be viewed as a person and not be bullied for the shoes I had on. I was aware of my blackness, and I was comfortable with myself.

My siblings and I could not understand why one black person bullied or laughed at another black person for being black. The culture at Eastway was a huge shock for us. The school had a large black population and other minority students. The Latinos were the second largest, but they never bothered us. Other minority students who attended school did not push us around like the black kids did. The black culture at school was not something we expected. At Eastway, the black kids were focused on the way they looked with specific shoes and baggy jeans. They skipped classes and went out behind trees to smoke cigarettes and marijuana. On numerous occasions, school had to be on shutdown (lock down) because someone brought a hand gun to school or was caught in possession of drugs. On the academic side, students at Eastway had the lowest performance in the whole Charlotte-Mecklenburg school system when it came to national standardized tests. This was the mess we were thrown into by Catholic Charities when we started school. Our case manager had no choice but to register us at this school because of where we resided, but it was horrible to say the least. School zoning in America is politically designed, and our home address fell in a zone that held us hostage.

My brother Maywal and I were not immune to peer pressure at school. We became convinced that the only way to be like the cool kids was to fit in. As a result, we wanted to look cool, to fit in the culture we found at Eastway. Therefore, we found the best way to do it was without our parents' notice. Maywal and I wore the fake gold chains and the baggy clothes and tried our best to be as cool as we could be. We sagged our pants every day as soon as we reached school. We pretended to be tougher than we were in order to make friends and scare off some of the kids who bullied us. One day, we were on the bus heading to school when a tall, skinny, light-skinned kid called "Big Mike" started to pick on us. Then a random student from the back of the bus said, "Them African dudes are lions. You don't wanna mess with them bros." Mike heard the warning loud and clear and got scared and kept his mouth shut. When we got off the bus that day, we felt like the toughest kids in the world without saying a word or throwing a punch at anyone.

That day my brother and I walked home from our bus stop, and we laughed about how that one kid got scared. In our laughter, we forgot to pull up our pants before reaching the house. We did not notice our mother watching as we walked up to the house. For the first time, she saw us looking like thugs with sagging pants. As we entered through the front door, she came behind us with a leather belt. We saw the belt hoovering over our heads and felt a strong wind-like force coming at us. We got a good spanking that day for sagging our pants. Mum had seen us, and she was not amused by what she saw that day. She certainly was not happy with the culture we were getting ourselves into at school. It was not the life she wanted for any of her boys.

At Eastway, Maywal and I learned a quick history about how sagging came into existence. According to a kid named William, pants sagging was started by males in federal correctional facilities many years ago. At that time, people who had been in prison for ten to fifteen years lost a lot of weight, so they walked around with their pants worn below the waist. This was the era of Tupac, Biggie, and other rappers. Because they wore saggy pants, sagging had become a thing of fashion. It was all about the bling and the baggy jeans, about being "hardcore" to look tough and cool.

Our next-door neighbor Willy told us a different version of the story. He said, "Pants sagging started in prison several years ago. It was a sign that one inmate was the 'girlfriend' of another and that he was willing to sleep with another man. Over time, it became a gang signal, and the color of the boxers that were showing indicated which gang the guy belonged to." Willy's version of the story was dirty, but nothing made me pull my pants up faster than the woman who had a vision for her boys, especially when she angrily told us, "I did not cross the Atlantic Ocean to sacrifice my life for you guys to have this kind of life!" Her words were powerful, and they began to shape me because I kept hearing her voice echoing in my head every time I wore my pants below the waist. I don't know if that touched Maywal like it did with me, but subconsciously her words hit me harder than two versions of the history. I have come to believe that sagging pants is a lack of self-respect, the embrace of thug life and prison culture, which was not part of my culture.

While my brother Maywal and I were at Eastway, we participated in sports. Maywal played on the soccer team his second year and was able to make new friends. Later that year, I followed Maywal's footsteps and played on the team also. Our teammates came from countries such as Somali, Bosnia, Russia, Mexico, Congo, and others. Our love for soccer was incredibly fascinating, and we had a strong team. Being a part of this team made us want to go to school more to meet our friends. In 2002, Maywal graduated from Eastway Middle School and attended Independence High School in the fall. That left me alone at Eastway, but by that time I had made lots of friends. In 2003, I tried out for the American football team out of curiosity. I was tired of soccer and wanted to try something different. I must admit that I loved playing American football. I became a kicker, punter, wide receiver, and a defensive end for Eastway football team. In May 2003, I graduated from Eastway Middle School, and my parents were not sure which school I should attend in the fall.

Thankfully, Mrs. Kim Schick, who befriended our family in 2003, helped us get into Myers Park High School. She was my younger brother's Sunday school teacher at St. Patrick's Catholic Church. She had children our ages, and one of her daughters started school at Myers Park that same year, and she knew it was a great school. She was a teacher with inside knowledge about how Charlotte-Mecklenburg Schools (CMS) operated. My parents did not know which schools were good or bad. As far as academic standing, in 2003, *Newsweek* magazine ranked Myers Park seventh among the country's top 1,050 high schools (WBTV 2008). Unlike Myers Park, Eastway Middle School had a low academic standing when my siblings and I attended. Unlike Eastway, which was mainly black and other minorities, Myers Park had predominately affluent whites with just a small number of minorities on campus. My brother and I were able to spot each other from a distance. The four students with African backgrounds who attended were Tesfom Mhari from Eritrea, a girl from Liberia, and my brother and me. The culture at school was different, and students were friendly. The staff was very professional and helpful. We were never bullied by the white kids during our high school years, and that helped us focus on our education. We got a lot of help from our teachers at Myers Park.

Our freshman year at Myers Park was a remarkable transition from a predominantly black school to a predominately white school. My brother and I did experience a culture shock at Myers Park, just as we did when we started school at Eastway. We were worried about everything, from feeling different to feeling isolated to experiencing the consequences of racism in a predominately white school. We didn't know what to expect. Myers Park was our first experience to really interact with the white kids and be exposed to a culture that was radically different from what we had experienced. But our worries disappeared as time passed, and we started to make more friends.

At Myers Park, my brother and I played football. I tried out for quarterback, and he went for wide receiver. We had fun playing football as we explored our new experience. I also joined the Junior Reserve Officers' Training Corps (JROTC) as a proud member of the Mustang Battalion. Through JROTC, I learned about discipline, leadership, and active citizenship. Joining JROTC profoundly affected my direction in life. As a cadet at Myers Park, Major Willie Douglas and First Sergeant George Powell were my instructors.

Our family friend Mrs. Schick volunteered several times at Myers Park. I saw her several times at the main office. She often checked on us to make sure we were doing well academically. She knew some of our teachers and was always there to help us if we had any issues. She was like our adopted mother who looked after us just like she did with her own children. When my mother could not make it to quarterly parent-teacher conferences because of her work schedule, Mrs. Schick went to those conferences on my mother's behalf to discuss our academic progress with our teachers. Since 2003, Mrs. Schick and her family have been great friends to our family. She assisted my mother with us when it came to school activities. On several occasions, she gave me rides home after football practice when it was her turn to carpool for her children. She also paid personally for a tutor to help me with math homework.

In 2006, my sister Amal graduated from high school. Amal can read, write, and speak Arabic fluently. She was educated in the US and is my only sister with a formal education. Her dream was to be a doctor, but that has not happened. At age seventeen, Amal got pregnant in her junior year of high school. She ruined her own dream by starting a family at a young age in a country where opportunities are tremendous. My mother was very disappointed with Amal for allowing a foolish man to ruin her future. As a result, she was out of school for a while until my mother encouraged her to continue her education. She went on and attended Grand Rapids Community College (GRCC) in Michigan but never got further in terms of education because she had to look after her own family.

In 2008, Maywal and I graduated from Myers Park High School. The feeling was great—it was a big achievement for both us. When our names were called out over the load speaker to get our high school diplomas, my mother, Uncle Moses (my mother's cousin) and his family, and friends were all cheering for us. My mother was our biggest cheerleader that day among the crowd. Our graduation was a remarkable experience, and she was extremely proud to see her children receive their diplomas. She expected us to go even further by going to college. Throughout our high school years, our mother always knocked on our doors in the morning to make sure we were up for school, even though we were old enough to get up on our own.

In 2014, Makot graduated from Myers Park High School. We attended his graduation, and it was another great experience for my mother to watch her youngest child receive his high school diploma. My brothers and I are all Myers Park High School graduates, except for Amoe who dropped out of school.

After we graduated from high school, the next step was to go to college. However, my parents did not have the money. So I enrolled in Central Piedmont Community College (CPCC) in uptown Charlotte while I worked part time at Moe's Southwest Grill. I was able to get financial aid for my first semester. Mrs. Schick encouraged me to apply for a Wilimore Neighborhood Association College Scholarship. This scholarship opportunity was offered to disadvantaged students in the community. "Bol, you have the grades, the story, and the leadership skills that you gained through JROTC. I am sure you will get it," she told me. I have always admired Mrs. Schick's confidence in me and her unyielding support. I applied and was awarded a $1,750 scholarship a month later, which I used toward my education at CPCC.

On June 7, 2010, I won another Wilimore Scholarship that was worth $2,000 and was incredibly humbled to have been chosen as a winner a second time around. The amount was minor in terms of money, but I was so thankful to have had such a wonderful resource to use toward my education. While I was attending CPCC, I enrolled in the Army Reserve Officers' Training Program (ROTC) at the University of North Carolina at Charlotte (UNC Charlotte). Around that time, I also took the test to become a US citizen and proudly passed it the first time. In addition, I worked at Moe's Southwest Grill to assist our family with bills. Sometimes working at Moe's interfered with my studies, but I continued to stay focused.

It was not an easy task to attend school, work, and participate in ROTC. Every day, I woke up at 5 a.m. and drove to UNC Charlotte for army physical training (PT). Then I drove back home to shower and get ready for my 8:30 a.m. class at CPCC. In the afternoon, I drove back to UNC Charlotte for an ROTC leadership course at 2:30 p.m. After school, I drove straight to work at Moe's. I'd be home by 10:30 p.m. It was a tough schedule, but I knew it was worthwhile.

At the University of North Carolina at Charlotte, I set my sights on an Army ROTC Scholarship. The scholarships that I previously won back-to-back gave me the confidence to aim at the prestigious army scholarship. I knew winning the ROTC scholarship would be competitive and hard to get, but I wanted it more than anyone else. That scholarship would best fit my financial needs and my desire to be commissioned as an Army officer once I graduated, and it would remove the financial burden of my education from my parents. The application was a lengthy process—one could even say that applying for it was half the battle toward receiving one!

What makes ROTC scholarships hard to receive is the fact that individual battalions do not control the scholarship or the source of funding. The process is all done by Cadet Command in Washington, DC. In order to be competitive, a cadet who wishes to apply must have an 1180 or higher SAT score, a 25 or higher ACT score, and a 3.0 to 4.0 grade point average, be clear medically, and score 180 or above on the army physical fitness test. I met all the test requirements, cleared medically, and had a 3.0 grade point average. After I applied for the scholarship, I crossed my fingers, prayed, and waited patiently. I put everything on God!

In fall 2010, I got a letter of admission into Belmont Abbey College. I received the news with great excitement, but I still did not know how I was going to pay for my education. Three weeks passed, and I still had not heard from the Army ROTC department. The process was taking too long. I began to worry, and doubts threatened to ruin my positive energy. One day while I was at the ROTC building, I finally found my name on the list of Army ROTC Scholarship recipients. I received that news with great joy and a sense of accomplishment. I could not wait to get home and share this news with my mother. I was incredibly grateful to have been among the five cadets chosen out of fifteen in our university who applied for the scholarship and many others at the national level. I felt like my hard work and faith had prepared me to embark on a new journey! As my mother once told us, "If you want something in life, go get it and be ready to hustle for it because nothing is easy. You have to struggle for it."

The scholarship required me to maintain a grade point average of 2.5 or higher each semester, meet army physical fitness standards, attend a thirty-day intense Leader Development and Assessment Course (LDAC), successfully complete LDAC or Warrior Forge (another leadership program), and successfully complete the Army ROTC program, after which I would enter the US Army at the rank of second lieutenant and serve for at least eight years.

Finally, in spring 2010, I began attending Belmont Abbey College on the full ride the Army ROTC Scholarship provided. Belmont Abbey College is a small, private, Benedictine Catholic institution located in Belmont, North Carolina. The Abbey is approximately ten miles west of Charlotte, and it's the only Catholic Benedictine college in the southeast and the only Catholic college throughout the Carolinas. I applied to Belmont Abbey College right after high school, but I did not get the acceptance immediately. I'm glad I did not get the offer immediately because there was no way I could afford it. It's all God's plans.

I learned about Belmont Abbey College through Mrs. Schick. I was drawn to the Abbey by my Catholic faith, and I discovered that I learned better in a small-classroom setting. After spending three years at the Abbey, I discovered that the college does a good job of improving mind, body, and soul through sharing the Catholic faith. I enjoyed attending student mass with friends and loved the intellectual debate in theology class with both professors and peers. The Abbey also reminded me to smile, meet new people, and just learn new things. My best memory at the Abbey was having the opportunity to invite Dr. Bill Thierfelder, the college president, to the ROTC Military Ball as a special guest. For him to accept my invitation was a great honor. I served as ROTC Company Commander for the college while participating in the student government.

Finally, in 2013, it was time to exit college and walk into the real world. Our graduation was done in front of the basilica at Belmont Abbey College. Rain was forecast, which would mean the graduation would be rescheduled, but by the grace of God, it did not rain on that special day. On May 11, 2013, I graduated from Belmont Abbey College with a bachelor's degree in political science and a minor in military science. It was the happiest day in my life. When my name was read aloud in the front of the crowd, I walked across the stage with confidence and joy, reached for my college diploma with my left hand, and shook the hands of college board members and the college president with my right. Then I walked off the stage and saw my family cheering me on. My mother was there, and she was so proud—words can't express her happiness and joy. I paused for a second and pointed toward my mother with a big smile on my face. I walked to my seat and had a conversation with myself. I was a kid who entered American school unable to speak English and now I was a college graduate. The journey was remarkable, to say the least.

My college degree symbolized victory for my hard work. It meant a lot to me and my family. I was the first in our family's history to go to college and receive a higher education from an excellent private college. I have come a long way on my education journey, and the source of my motivation was my mother who never had the full education she wanted. Mum was the one I thought about from the time my name was called to the time I had my degree in my hand. She sacrificed everything she had for me to come this far. It was my mother's dream to see her children have the education she never had. For her to see me walk across the stage that day was a huge victory in her life. I owed that degree to her, and I will never forget how blessed my life has been with her unyielding support.

In 2016, I visited South Sudan and was able to see the need for education across the country. I was able to buy notebooks and pencils to give to the students. This gave children and their parents a sign that hope can be restored in the face of a hopeless situation that prevents children from reaching their potential. As a child who really understood my mother's thirst for education, I did not want to limit myself to academic excellence in just my own educational journey. I want to extend my mother's dream to less fortunate children in her village and in South Sudan as a whole one day.

After I returned to the United States, I started a project to build a school in Aweil, South Sudan. I bought t-shirts to sell with "Educating Panjab 2017" written on them. This was my attempt to spread awareness and raise funds for the cause. This project means a lot to me because I want to bring education to my mother's village, where her hunger for education started. I made a promise to the children of Panjab village that I will do my part to make sure a school becomes a reality. The school will be named after my grandfather who founded Panjab village, but it will be a gift to the community. Building a school there is on my priority list, and I will work hard to see it achieved.

My siblings and I are privileged and grateful to have attended school in America. Unfortunately, not all of them achieved the academic success my mother expected. My siblings fell short of her expectations, but I continue to strive to fulfill her dream to the best of my ability. I won numerous scholarships in my educational journey and continue to exceed my mother's expectations.

In 2016, I applied for another scholarship to further my education and to seek new opportunities. My friend Patricia Shafer, whom I had known for more than three years, encouraged me to apply for the Rotary Peace Fellowship. I applied and was nominated by Rotary District 7680 as a candidate. I was lucky to have a small team of wonderful people from District 7680 who saw my potential and supported me in the application process. Each year, the Rotary Foundation offers up to fifty fellowships for master's degrees and fifty for certificate studies at premier universities. Candidates must demonstrate excellent leadership skills and strong commitment to international understanding and peace through professional and academic achievement and personal or community service.

As someone who came from a family that survived civil war and lived as a refugee for several years, I was determined not only to further my education but also to find a way to make a difference. The Rotary Peace Fellowship was my chance to work for peace in South Sudan. That is the least I can do for a country that fought so hard for liberation. The United States government supports South Sudan in numerous ways, including implementing the Comprehensive Peace Agreement (CPA) that formally ended twenty-two years of conflict. My family members who fought in the civil war invested so much to liberate South Sudan, and it cannot be allowed to fail.

When I discovered that I was selected to receive the Rotary Peace Scholarship in November 2016, I was extremely excited for the opportunity. My mother is the motivation that pushed me to strive for excellence because it's her that I want to make proud. My accomplishments are a result of my own work ethic and my mother's expectations of me. I learned that success is a product of skill and drive. And I was motivated by the fact that education is the most powerful weapon that can be used to bring about positive change in the world.

As a young military leader, this was an opportunity to learn about international relations, peace, conflict, development, and security from an international perspective. After obtaining my master's degree in peace and conflict-related studies, I would be able to advance as an Army officer at a more senior level. My Army commanders encouraged my desire to obtain a master's degree and supported me when I stated my intention to further my education. They were well aware of the direct relevance and prestige of a Rotary Peace Fellowship. The path was cleared for me to fully participate in the program with a transfer of my US Army military service requirements to an overseas environment. Luckily, I did not have to serve while undertaking the rigorous academic course load and resumed my military service upon my return to the United States.

I was offered the position to study at the Rotary Peace Center at the University of Bradford in West Yorkshire, UK. On August 23, 2017, I arrived in the United Kingdom for my studies. The Division of Peace and International Development at Bradford is internationally recognized as a center for excellence in research, teaching, training, and policy engagement. My area of concentration was in peace, conflict, and development studies, integrating theory and applied practice. As someone who was trained to kill in the US Army, the Rotary Peace Fellowship training provided a different perspective. As a peace scholar, I was trained to apply rigorous research and learning to the challenge of conflict globally. Through research and applying theories, the training provided extensive and in-depth knowledge related to international, national, and local social, political, and economic dynamics that lead to war.

On a personal level, the chance to study in the UK was an opportunity to embark on a personal quest to find solutions to the current South Sudanese conflict and prevent future conflicts by understanding the mechanism to sustain peace through my advanced professional education. I believe that this line of study and inquiry will also add to my ability to help the country where my mother was born. South Sudan, which became a new, independent country on July 9, 2011, is widely considered among the poorest and most fragile countries in this world. This is not an accident. These dire circumstances are a legacy of prolonged and extreme conflict exacerbated by an irresponsible use of military and militia forces along ethnic lines.

When I returned to South Sudan in 2016, the political instability, corruption, and insecurity that I witnessed was disturbing to say the least. This young country needs to be developed as a true nation through implementation of a lasting peace agreement that ordinary citizens deserve and the international community should more actively support and implement. For my master's dissertation, I envisioned a line of research in which I outlined potential approaches by which the current South Sudan military and opposition leaders could reposition themselves as a force for peace and development.

Personally, I believe that achieving lasting peace is possible in South Sudan. I have long understood the importance of peace because of my firsthand experiences during the Second Sudanese Civil War and as a child living in refugee camps. Globalist Paddy Ashdown once said, "Today, in our modern world, because of the Internet, everything is connected to everything. We are now interdependent. We are now interlocked as nations, as individuals, in a way which has never been the case before." One of the greatest barriers to peace in the world is the fact that mankind does not understand that all humans share a collective destiny. Peace, conflict, and development studies at Bradford helped me build a career that aligns with and reinforces these values. I am confident that I can and will live up to the hopes and expectations that go along with the values of Rotary International and the generous support of the Rotary Peace Fellowship. It's my desire to use my education to contribute to a more peaceful world.

On December 6, 2019, I graduated from the University of Bradford with a master's degree in peace, conflict, and development. I completed my studies with an overall merit and earned a mark of distinction on my master's dissertation, which focused on South Sudan's fragility, elite competition, and myths. Shortly after graduation, I called my mother to share this achievement and to remind her that such high achievement was possible due to her high expectation of me. I became the first person in my family's history to earn both a bachelor's and a master's degree and have my education paid for through scholarships. My mother is proud to see me come this far!

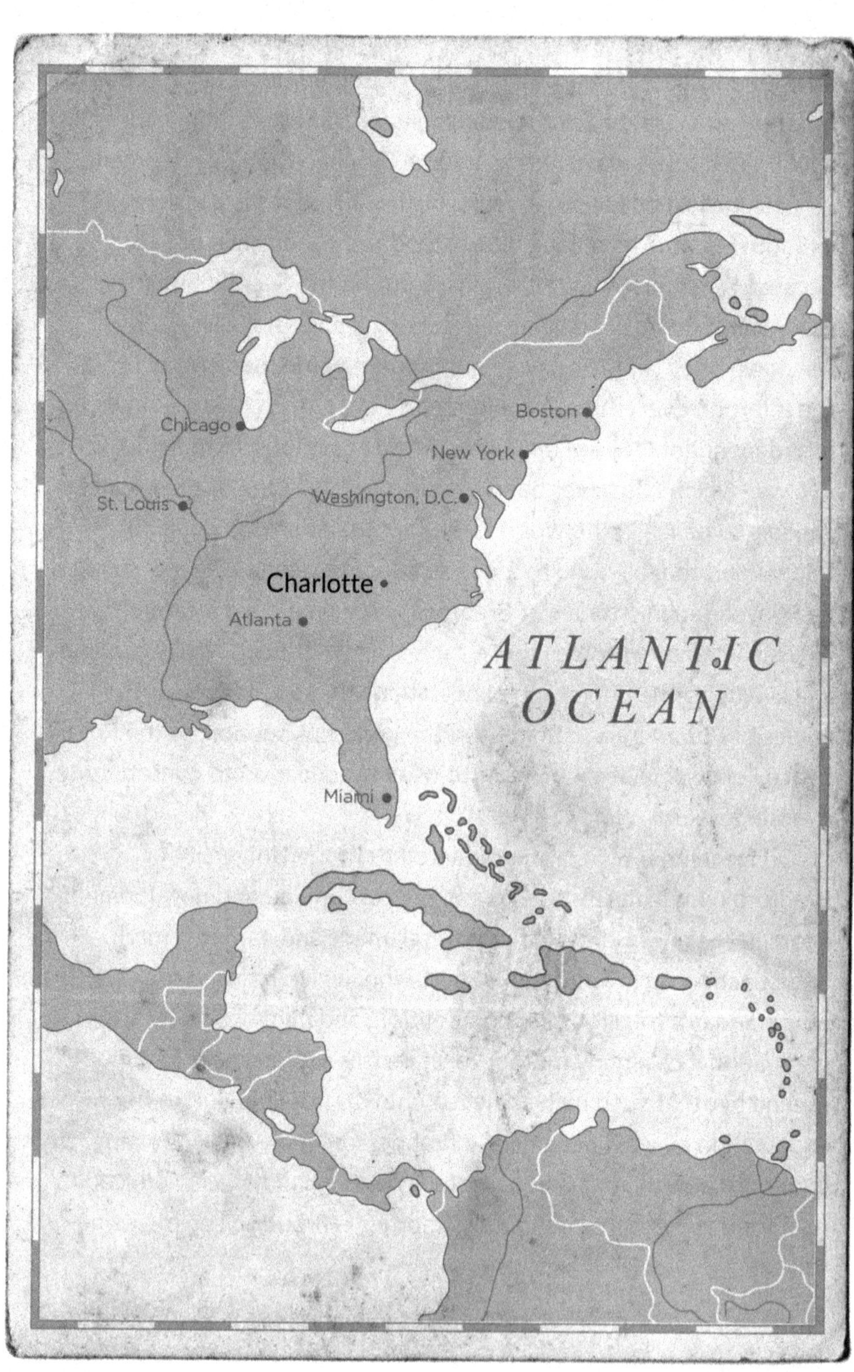

Chicago
Boston
New York
St. Louis
Washington, D.C.
Charlotte
Atlanta
ATLANTIC
OCEAN
Miami

A Future Leader

Thank you for giving me a shot at the American dream.

– Second Lieutenant Alix Idrache, upon graduation from the United States Military Academy at West Point

As long as I can remember, I have wanted to serve others. Leadership was where I found my passion. My parents noticed that in me from an early age. I remember telling my mother that one day I would be a great soldier and leader.

At the refugee camp, I heard stories about my uncles who fought during the two Sudanese civil wars. My mother's half-brother, Ungua Goi Ungua, was conscripted in 1940 by the colonial ruler (Britain) and fought in World War II alongside Allied forces against the Italians in the East African Campaign. When the Italian communication code was cracked, the British forces—made up of British colonies—launched an offensive from Sudan and Kenya. By 1941, after months of fighting, they pushed back the Italian forces at the Battle of Gondar in Ethiopia. At the end of the war in 1941, he never returned to his village. He was killed on the front line, according to my mother.

Uncle Lual Goi Ungua also fought in the First Sudanese Civil War. He later returned to his village after the war and is currently serving as a village chief. Like Uncle Lual, Mum's younger brother, also named Ungua, fought as a child soldier when he joined the Sudan People's Liberation Army (SPLA), a guerilla army that fought against the oppressive Islamic regime that burned Panjab village to ashes during the Second Sudanese Civil War.

I was inspired by my uncles' bravery and their sacrifices to liberate their people from the yoke of Arab domination. My uncle and others gave their youth and energy to fight in order to free elderly, children, and women who were defenseless. Their selfless service had the greatest influence on me as a boy in the refugee camp where my motivation to serve others started. I always wanted to be a soldier to serve others as a guardian of peace and freedom.

Like my mother, the entire family was traumatized by the Sudanese civil wars and the oppression under Arab rule in Sudan. I grew up with hatred towards Arabs, and when I reached teenage years, that resentment continued to grow. I could not wait to grow up and fight the enemies who destroyed my mother's village, killed 2.5 million southern Sudanese, and forced thousands to become refugees. Four years of mistreatment by Arab Egyptians in Cairo, Egypt, further fueled my bitterness toward Muslims and Arabs. Then the horrors of the 9/11 attack on American soil, which I witnessed as a boy, exacerbated my motivation to want to kill those who threaten peace and security, especially against unarmed civilians. At that time, I was motivated by revenge, although I grew into a mission of peace through my studies.

At age sixteen, I joined the Junior Reserve Officers' Training Corps (JROTC) at Myers Park High School as a part of my leadership development journey. The mission of JROTC is "to motivate young people to be better citizens." It teaches discipline, personal courage, honor, respect, and other leadership skills.

On the first week, all the cadets were issued books, shoes, uniforms, and equipment. When I came home with all of my gear, my mother almost had a heart attack the moment she saw military equipment in my hands. She thought I had joined the military without parental approval! "You know we fled Sudan because of brutal civil war, and you decided to join the military to go to war? Are you crazy?" she asked me. I told her that I did not join the military yet and that I was only a cadet. I explained to her that the mission of JROTC was to motivate and equip young people to practice active citizenship.

I completely understood where she was coming from with all her worries. My mother saw people in her village shot dead at point-blank range and her husband killed when her village was attacked. And her youngest brother who served in the Sudan People's Liberation Army (SPLA) returned home in 2005 with post-traumatic stress disorder (PTSD). Although we had been living in the US for over four years, my mother was still traumatized by the civil war experience. Indeed, we were new in America, and the US had invaded Iraq and Afghanistan, and the two wars raged on. Mum thought I would be sent to the front line because I enrolled in JROTC. Although I found this laughable, I was able to educate my mother about JROTC and told her that everything would be alright. Her worries disappeared when I told her I had no military obligation as a cadet. I reminded my mother that my dream was to be a soldier like my uncles. I told her the Islamic fundamentalists that my uncles fought were the same enemy the US was fighting. "What difference would it make if I fought these enemies as an American soldier?" I asked her. She went silent for a moment and then told me that I was too young to join the military.

I took JROTC seriously because I knew it was something worth doing. I was determined to learn, and I assumed leadership roles on numerous occasions. My first leadership position was as a team leader, and my responsibilities consisted of keeping accountability of all personnel, disseminating information to my team members, and inspecting the uniforms of my team. After I successfully completed all my responsibilities, I was assessed among my peers and was considered for the platoon leader position. In my senior year, I received the Senior Leadership Award for demonstrating outstanding

leadership qualities. I was a cadet for over two years, and I loved
the Army JROTC program very much. While in the Army JROTC, I
became convinced that my life calling was to serve others.

I followed through with the idea of wanting to serve the country
that gave my family opportunities we never had in Africa. In August
2009 while still at Central Piedmont Community College, I enrolled
in Reserve Officers' Training Corps (ROTC) at the University of
North Carolina at Charlotte in order to get my commission as an
Army officer. The Army ROTC is one of the most demanding and
successful leadership programs in universities across the country.
The Army ROTC teaches leadership development, military skills,
and career training to prepare cadets for complex world situations. I
took rigorous, advanced leadership courses in the classroom and in
the field.

When I turned twenty years old during my sophomore year in
college, my mother supported my desire to continue with Army
ROTC when she realized that all the military training I had received
in ROTC had built me into a solid soldier and leader. "Since you are
passionate about wanting to be a leader, I will share some of the
leadership traits that your grandfather had," she once told me. My
grandfather was a well-respected village chief and known as a man
of peace because he was able to keep peace among different ethnic
groups through his leadership. My mother was her dad's favorite
child, so she had the privilege of watching her dad lead others. She
shared his leadership traits with me.

"There are six traits you need to know if you want to lead," she
said. "People will follow if a leader has the following: foresight,
passion, courage, wisdom, generosity, and trustworthiness." Since
she noticed that I was very passionate about wanting to lead,
she added, "Passion does not necessarily indicate being loud or
charismatic about things; it indicates depth and determination.
People in need of help are always eager to follow a leader who is
deeply committed to their cause. A good leader does not do things
for personal benefits in order to get a 'shiny object' for reward. A

good leader will always put people first and follow through in order to deliver to the people."

Aside from passion, Mum said courage is essential in leadership: "A good leader is someone who can make tough decisions in difficult times. Leaders often must make decisions that are personally uncomfortable but are for the greater good of the people. To a leader, the people are more important than personal comfort. As a leader, one must be wise in order to discern or judge what is true or false before making decisions." Then she shared an old African proverb that says, "If you are filled with pride, then you will have no room for wisdom."

She continued, "Leaders must have the ability to think deeply. They see patterns in the problems that need an answer and share them with their advisors, which allows them together to make the moral choice. Speed in action is often commended, but thinking deeply about controversial issues and making decisions that are taken seriously and aren't spur of the moment is more commendable, especially in a leader. Patience is the path that solves all problems because it gives you time to think before taking action. Nobody is born wise, but understanding the problem is winning half the battle."

The fifth element that a leader ought to have is generosity. The quality of being kind and generous toward all people will take you far in life. "Generosity in leadership is not mainly about material wealth," my mother would say, "as leaders do also have to be cautious when it comes to community resources and national wealth. But that's not to say one cannot be generous in spirit, with praise, hope, faith, information, responsibility, and political or military power. When leaders believe in their people and support their success, that's the best kind of generosity that the citizens would love to see."

While listening to Mum, I tried to absorb as much as I could from what she observed from the "old man," my grandfather. Nowadays, leaders tend to forget about the people who put them in power, especially in African countries where the majority of those in leadership positions are consumed by greed of power and material wealth. Mum told me, "Never allow money, women, or power to change you, son, in anything you do!"

The final thing you need to always keep in the back of your head is trust, according to Mum. "People must know that you are a trustworthy person in order for them to do what you ask of them," she would say and then elaborate a little about trust. "Your grandfather was chief of a small village for a long time because people trusted him. Historically, leaders were elected to provide protection to a group—a family, a community, a kingdom, or a nation. When people don't trust a leader to protect the group, they would feel like they had to protect themselves; and when a group is self-protected, it's difficult to interact freely when lack of trust exists. When it comes to making a good leader, none of the other traits I mentioned earlier can exist without the rest, but trust is foundational to leadership. When people trust a leader, they trust his or her character and his or her competence. Someone capable of leading as well as competent to do the job gives people faith in him or her. Like respect, trust is earned, son. Always know that!"

Later, during my college career, I was appointed company commander for Belmont Abbey College by Lieutenant Colonel McGinnis, the chairman of military science. As a commander, I was responsible for all the cadets in the Belmont Abbey ROTC programs for three years. My duties included mentoring junior cadets, scheduling training, and more. Aside from being a cadet and commander in ROTC, I was involved in the Student Government Association and served as a senator for two years.

Finally, in 2013, immediately after graduating from Belmont Abbey College, the dream that I had as a nine-year-old was realized. On May 10, 2013, during our commissioning ceremony, I raised my right hand to take the oath of office as an Army officer before the American people and my peers. I was honored to have Major Willie Douglas swear me in as an officer. After I took the oath of office, my mother and my brother Allah-jabo came forward to pin the gold bar of a second lieutenant on each shoulder. When my mother pinned

the insignia on my shoulder, my voice choked with emotion, and I
came close to shedding tears knowing the struggle my mother went
through to raise me and bring me to this moment. It was a very
emotional moment for both of us.

My Mum was so proud and happy that day that she raised her
voice in the traditional "la-la" noise that southern Sudanese women
often do on a special day. It was so uplifting and special to me. I knew
she was celebrating her hard work for raising a young man to be a
leader. My mother was so happy because she knew how I struggled
to get to that big day. She also knew her dreams for my success and
opportunities and her own struggle to raise me to become the young
man I am. Her dream became reality when she knew that I will never
let her down. I understand her pain and sacrifices, and everything I
want to do and accomplish in life, I owe to her. I saw my mother's
happiness, and it was like a beacon, lighting up the future for me with
all her blessings.

After I was pinned, the crowd erupted with applause to
congratulate me and my peers, newly commissioned United States
Army officers. "Congratulations, lieutenant! You did it, man, and I
am proud of you!" said Major Willie. "Thank you, sir!" I replied as we
shook hands. After the swearing-in ceremony, I received my first
salute as an officer from a Vietnam veteran, First Sergeant George
Powell, US Army (Ret.). Major Willie and First Sergeant Powell
were my Army JROTC instructors at Myers Park High School. I had
promised them back then when I was under their leadership that once
I completed my Army ROTC program at a university level, I would
invite them to be a part of this special event. That was a promise I was
proud to keep.

That commissioning day was the biggest accomplishment of my
life. That gold bar of a second lieutenant means leadership in the US
Army, and it's not just given randomly. It must be earned through
rigorous training that requires physical and mental toughness
and taking an oath before the American people. Leading the sons
and daughters of the United States of America is not a right, but

a privilege and serious business. I earned it through sweat and
hard work.

To be an officer is to be respected as a professional soldier and an
inspiring leader. After I received my commission, I was assigned to
my first unit where I was in charge of other soldiers, men and women
who potentially would be older than I was. This task was a challenge
for a twenty-two-year-old, but I was confident and determined. I
put all the leadership and military skills that I gained throughout my
academic years in college and my ROTC career and applied them in
the real world. Officers are the leaders of the Army, and they lead
from the front and adjust to an environment that is always changing.
I was ready to lead, and I was ready to take on any challenge. The
ROTC program instilled in me a deep sense of gratitude and an
obligation to give back to this great nation. I thank all my commanders
and the American people for giving me a shot at the American dream.

From left to right: Adout Goi Ungua, Bol Maywal, and Allah-jabo Maywal share a smile with fellow Americans after Bol was pinned as a second lieutenant in the US Army. *Photo by Mr. Curtis Lawrence, UNC Charlotte Army ROTC Office Manager.*

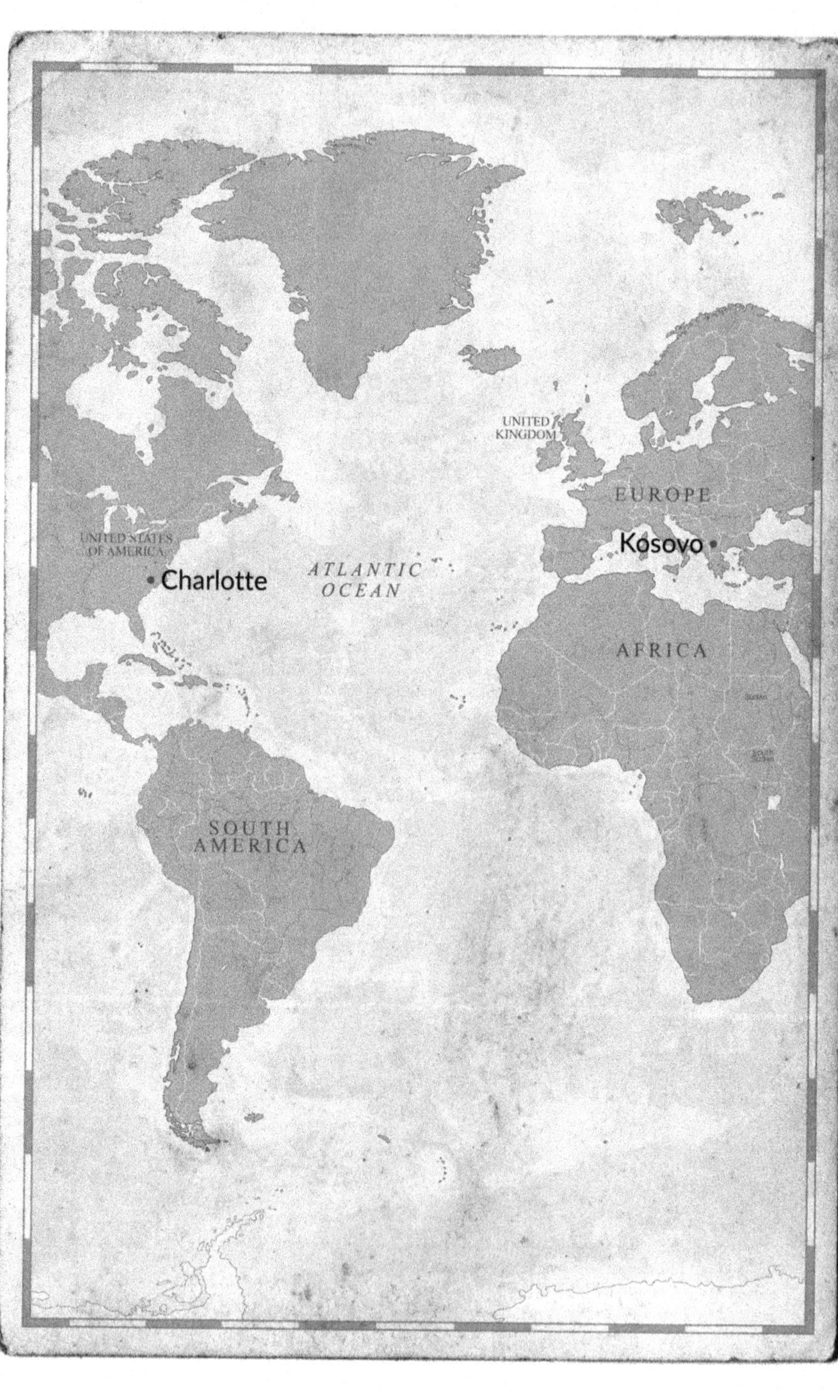

UNITED
KINGDOM
EUROPE
Kosovo
UNITED STATES
OF AMERICA
Charlotte
ATLANTIC
OCEAN
AFRICA
SOUTH
AMERICA

CHAPTER 10

Unsung Hero

**Do not withhold good from
those to whom it is due, when
it is in your power to act.**

– Proverbs 3:27 (NIV)

My mother is definitely my kindness champion. She is literally the nicest person and most thoughtful woman I have ever met. When we lived in the displacement camp, my stepfather imposed a strict curfew that forced us to be home before 5 p.m. One day, we were out playing soccer with friends and didn't notice we were running late. When we came home later after the game, my stepfather was already there ready to deal with us.

"Where were you guys at?" he asked.

"We were out playing soccer," my cousin replied. Maywal and I were silent, which left our cousin, who was older than both of us, to answer.

"Well, I hope you guys enjoyed the game. No dinner for the three of you tonight, so don't waste your time waiting around," my stepfather told us. We took his orders like soldiers and disappeared from his sight. Of course, we were disappointed that we had to go to bed with empty stomachs, but we could not disobey the orders.

Our punishment for not being back home on time really bothered me. Food was scarce in the displacement camp, and I could not believe my stepfather would force us kids to go to bed without dinner. Maywal and my cousin were probably thinking the same. My stepfather walked over to Mum and said, "The boys violated the curfew, so do not serve them food tonight." We heard that loud and clear, so we didn't waste our time and took our blankets off to bed.

Around 10 p.m., my Mother came and woke us up and asked us to stay quiet as she served us food. We were surprised because Mum had always respected my stepfather's authority. We looked over where our stepfather was sleeping; he was knocked out sleeping and snoring. We wanted to laugh so hard that night, but we did not want to get Mum in trouble. It was funny how that night had turned out for us. Thanks to Mum, we were able to sleep with full bellies. We laughed as much as we could the next morning at school and shared the story with friends, who laughed along with us.

Mum was kind not only to us but also to strangers, and she never felt awkward. During the time my family lived in the displacement camp in Sudan and later as refugees in Egypt, no one ever said anything negative about my mother. To this day, her friends and others come to her for help, and she will always reach out.

At the displacement camp, a woman who did not have enough maize flour to cook fufu to feed her children came to my mother. My mother went to the kitchen and gave the woman enough maize flour to feed her family for a week. When school started, one of her friend's children was denied admission to the local primary school because her mother was disabled and couldn't pay the fees. My mother gave the woman extra money to assist her child. Mum did this because she believed that one day that child would contribute to society. My family did not live beyond our means in the displacement camp. In fact, we were in the same miserable condition as those my mother often helped. It's hard to believe that she would go out of her way to help others given the condition the family was in, but she did it out of her kindness and generosity. She once told us, "The main rule to me is to honor the Almighty God with my life—living the life of integrity and not being selfish toward people in need of help. You all must learn to help others, but do not forget to help yourself first. When you have a little more than another person, you have the responsibility to help others."

One day in Jebel Aulia, my mother was on her way to pick up aid from the UN Distribution Centre when she ran into a woman giving birth near a rain-flooded area. The woman had been heading to the UN medical clinic, which was a long way to walk. She had to stop because the pain wouldn't allow her to continue. The baby's head was out, and the lady was near nasty water; the baby could have drowned as the mother squatted in an attempt to lie on her back. My mother rushed onto the scene when she heard the baby cry and the woman scream for help. Mum was in the right place at the right time. Despite these conditions, the lady was able to give birth to a healthy baby boy as Mum covered him up with her rain jacket to keep him as dry and warm as possible. The baby was later named Deng, meaning "rain" in Dinka dialect. My mother's skill as a midwife was vital at that moment, and she might have saved the lives of both mother and child. When my mother was a young girl, her mother took her to attend traditional births in the remote areas of southern Sudan. This allowed Mum to watch and learn how to assist other women giving birth.

Throughout her time in the displacement camps, Mum dedicated some of her time to serve as a midwife, helping to bring babies into this world. The harsh conditions and lack of electricity in the camp meant people relied on the natural light of the sun and moon. It was very dark in the camp at night. At one point, a young lady was sent to get my mother around 11:30 p.m. to help a woman who was delivering that night. Mum ran back to our house to grab the only kerosene lamp we had to make sure the baby was not harmed during the delivery.

Maternal mortality was a serious problem for women in the refugee camps, and Mum believed that a motherless baby begins life at a disadvantage. In addition to missing maternal love, the infant is at risk for malnourishment and other types of infections that babies are prone to. Mum understood this very well because she had experienced the harsh conditions herself with her own children. Like Deng's mother, Mum gave birth to my youngest brother, Makot, along a roadside.

My aunt, Mum's younger sister, was on trial in Islamic court. Her Muslim husband had falsely accused her of converting from Islam to Christianity, for which the penalty is death in countries under Islamic rule. Mum was traveling alone when she gave birth in an abandoned, partially constructed, three-story building in Khartoum. It was the only place Mum could find shade and cover to keep her cool and protect her privacy. But she was more worried about my aunt being hung than about herself dying from maternal mortality. Luckily, Mum was able to get help from a kind woman who happened to be passing by that day. My mother could have been among the many women who died from maternal mortality in the displacement camps.

Thanks to God, Mum was brave, and she got help. It's with this spirit that she volunteered her time to prevent maternal and newborn deaths. "It hurts my heart to watch any woman go through such agonizing pain at childbirth. However, it was an absolute honor to assist them and encourage them through the process," she said. At the refugee camps, my mother estimates she assisted more than 900 babies and their mothers during birth. No children or mothers died in childbirth on her watch.

My mother instilled in us at an early age the attitude of looking after others and not just ourselves. It was a requirement in her book. Personally, as her eighth child, the idea of lending a hand to others has stayed with me and has gotten me far in life. I was inspired by Mum's kindness and generosity toward perfect strangers, which had a strong influence on me, especially when she asked, "How would you feel if you were in a situation where you needed the assistance from someone, and that person chose to walk away? Put yourself in that situation and tell me how you would feel. Life is unpredictable, son, and you will never know if the person you are helping today could help you somewhere down the road." Being considerate or thoughtful of others is something that was taught to all her children, but it was already embedded into my DNA from her, as I later discovered.

In 2003, I started volunteering for Habitat for Humanity by lending a hand to build houses for many disadvantaged families. I was inspired by stories Mum shared with all of us about how others helped her in difficult times and how other people will never forget how you shape their lives by a touch of kindness. This same spirit drove me to volunteer on numerous occasions to make a difference in our community.

In spring of 2014, my mother returned to the Refugee Resettlement Office to see if they could assist her in finding a job. I went along with her to help interpret since her English was poor. There, I spotted Mr. Gull, who was our family case coordinator when we first arrived in the United States. I walked into his office to say hello, and we spoke briefly. I asked him if the office was hiring anytime soon. He told me that Alicia, who had worked there for over ten years, recently retired and that they would need someone to replace her. He encouraged me to talk to Mr. Ashir and Cira about a position.

At the time, I was serving in the Army National Guard while waiting to be sent to the Army's Basic Officer Leader Course (BOLC), so I could also hold a civilian job. I applied for the case coordinator position and was called for the first interview. I felt it went well and could not wait to join the organization, making a difference and bringing hope to people uprooted by conflict and persecution.

Finally, on May 2, 2014, I was offered the job to join Catholic Charities Diocese of Charlotte as a full-time case coordinator. I wanted to give back to this organization that sponsored my family years ago. I was super excited to get the job and ready to start! The office was near uptown Charlotte and only three minutes from my house. On my first day, my supervisor walked me to room number 286 and said, "You and Mr. Gull will work side by side in this office. There is your desk." Then he asked, "How does it feel to work alongside your former case coordinator, Mr. Gull?" It was surreal, and I was speechless. Then Mr. Gull chimed in. "He was a small boy when his family first came to the US; I remember him very well. It's an honor to work with such a fine young man," he said. I could have never imagined that one day I'd be sitting in the Refugee Resettlement Office to help other refugees resettle in the US. I was inspired because their stories were my own, and I knew the difficulties of the refugee camps in Burma, Somalia, Congo, Iraq, Syria, and Bhutan.

When I worked for Catholic Charities to assist those in need, I realized the meaning of "I am my brothers' (and sisters') keeper." It inspired me to work alongside great coworkers at the Refugee Resettlement Office who felt they could make a difference in the world. That was their motivation and their passion and what made me love working there every day. That passion to look out for others filled my heart and gave me purpose. I worked diligently to assist refugees become self-sufficient and self-reliant upon their arrival in the United States. I was able to use my exceptional organizational skills, leadership skills, educational background, and ability to work well with others to ensure success for all my clients. I came in each day and began the paperwork to enroll my clients in immigration and refugee services. I worked hard to ensure that clients received necessary support and information about community resources. I managed clients' finances, enrolled children in schools, assisted them with opening bank accounts, taught cultural orientation classes on weekends, and maintained a client caseload of twenty to forty clients annually.

The day my mother went to the refugee office to look for a job, I ended up getting a job. Had I not followed my mother that day to assist her, I would not have had the opportunity to work at the Refugee Resettlement Office. Thanks, Mum! It's all your blessing. I loved my job. I mean, I enjoyed my work as a case coordinator, but to make a difference in peoples' lives through advocacy and through a strong organization such as Charlotte Catholic Charities was the kind of privilege that few young people ever get. As a young case coordinator, I got to touch lives; I got to make a difference. As the old saying goes, you never have had a perfect day until you have done something for someone who will never pay you back. I have always had that burning desire to serve people and make a difference in the world.

Out of gratitude and a sense of service gained through my good fortune, I have become a dedicated volunteer to assist those less fortunate, often those who are victims of conflict. From 2004 through 2013, I volunteered for Habit for Humanity, lending a hand to build houses for disadvantaged families. The UN Universal Declaration of Human Rights lists safety and shelter as experiences to which every human being is entitled. I have lived the life of displacement and homelessness and have felt the despair of uncertainty associated with fleeing across open land and living in a makeshift home of straw and tarpaulin. Life in that refugee camp is galvanized in my memory. Once we got to Charlotte, volunteers helped build my family's first home through Habitat for Humanity. I was inspired and wanted to give back in return. I have also volunteered at the Habitat ReStore, stocking items, loading and unloading materials, answering phones, and assisting clients as they assemble baby cribs and sort through things of value. Through Catholic Charities, I have coordinated distribution from food pantries to newly arriving refugees and taught cultural orientation and assimilation classes. I have also volunteered as a spokesperson through projects that were started by Patricia Shafer, a Rotary Peace Fellow and founder of the Raising South Sudan Project.

In October 2014, I took leave from Catholic Charities to attend an Army Basic Officer Leader Course in Arizona. While there, one of my friends called and said, "Lieutenant Maywal, would you like to deploy to Kuwait with the unit and then as a liaison officer for the boss when you return to North Carolina?" I told her I would be more than happy to help, to deploy and serve my country in any capacity, but I had already been asked to deploy to Kosovo. "Sounds good, lieutenant. Let me know if you change your mind," she said. Two weeks before my graduation from my officer course, I got another request from the Joint Force Headquarters in Raleigh, North Carolina, asking me to deploy to Africa with our Special Force Unit. I said I would consider it and get back to them. I had three deployment requests waiting for me, but it was my choice to decide which one to take with which unit. This would be my first deployment, so I wanted to make sure to go to a place I had never been.

Finally, in 2015, I graduated from the Basic Officer Leader Course, one of the most demanding and intellectually challenging programs in the United States Army. Upon completion of this advanced leadership course, I volunteered for a NATO Peace Operation Mission in Kosovo. NATO had been leading a peace-support operation in Kosovo since 1999 as a core aspect of a wider international collaboration to build peace and stability in the Balkans. This was the first opportunity for me to make a real difference in the world. In Kosovo, our battle group was tasked with assisting reconstruction and demining, providing medical assistance, ensuring security and public order, protecting religious sites, providing border security, establishing civilian institutions, and providing law and order. At the tactical level, I was part of the team that provided advice and support to the Kosovo Security Force (KSF) at the brigade level and above. This involved focusing on staff capacity and building and training the Kosovo Security Force (KSF). The KSF was a new, professional, multiethnic, lightly armed, and uniformed security force that would soon assume responsibility for Kosovo's security as the security situation on the ground improved.

My work experience as a refugee case worker at Catholic Charities in Charlotte helped me understand the special needs of minorities that we encountered during the peacekeeping mission in Kosovo.

My commander tasked a team of soldiers, of which I was a part, to manage donations of food and school supplies to the locals, as well as to provide safety and security escort services during a community outreach event at Camp Bondsteel, Kosovo (Lt. Col. Buentello 2015). In this capacity, I worked with disadvantaged families, school children, teachers, and community spokespeople to build partnerships and friendships between the locals and NATO. Upon completion of my deployment in 2016, I was awarded the Non-Article 5 NATO Peace Medal for service of peace and freedom in Kosovo. This award reinforced my commitment to be a global agent of peace.

The life journey and experiences, from being a refugee myself to working closely with others, has fueled my passion to be further involved in peace and conflict resolution. My life in general, enhanced by my work and volunteer experiences, has fulfilled many of my parents' dreams and profoundly shaped my thinking for the future. The most distinct among my goals is to become a proactive agent of peace locally and globally. I have been trained to be an agent of war, a soldier. And as such, I understand conflict, killing, and abuse. Yet my life is bounded by another training—the life training of living as a refugee, fearing civil war, and the despair of having no future ahead. And I am blessed to know what it's like to live in America, a country where peace, justice, equality, and prosperity are the core of the national promise. My life's goal is to find a way for others to follow my path.

After graduating from the University of Bradford, I know that my career and personal pursuits will always involve humanitarian and nonprofit work, particularly in support of vulnerable populations. My mother has already suggested that at some point I should return to the Republic of South Sudan and consider serving in a public policy role as the country continues moving away from the conflicts of the past. I see that—with new insights from the Rotary Peace Fellowship—I can do this even more broadly in the larger East African Community to which South Sudan now belongs, including Kenya, Tanzania, Rwanda, Burundi, and Uganda. On an even larger and more strategic scale, I anticipate a career influencing policy and strategy regarding the positive role of the military in supporting stability and economic growth in some of the most precarious parts of the world.

Initially, I can do this within the roles I described above. After completing my military obligation, I can transition into civilian life and play a role of active citizenship. With a master's degree from the University of Bradford, I intend to enter politics and make a difference. In the longer term, I would be willing to serve in an appointed or elected office in South Sudan. It is my belief that the world needs civic leaders who value service, integrity, and courage to be a force for political unity rather than disunity. Today, we see political parties, communities, and nations at war with themselves and each other. I appreciate that my life experiences, as well as the insights and skills that I gained through a Rotary Peace Fellowship and related graduate studies, will present more opportunities to build bonds of connection and fellowship across geographies, cultures, and contexts.

The leadership skills that I gained through my military career have enhanced my ability to lead others in my community. My community volunteerism is not because it looks good on my resume or because of the praise received, but because I believe in our common humanity. A few hours donated to a charity organization can make a difference. True aid comes not from a forced government program, but from ordinary people crafting a brighter future for someone in need. It's with that mindset that I grow my sense of humanity, lest I become as poor in charity and compassion as those I help are poor in food or clothing. Strong commitment toward community-oriented service is a step toward a brighter future for all.

When I visited South Sudan in 2016, I discovered from the villagers that my mother is a hero. Hollywood movies often portray heroes in spectacular ways. Unlike the heroes portrayed in movies, unsung heroes are ordinary people who do extraordinary things by trying their best to help others. In the process, they persist through struggles and act heroically without the elements of a fantasy world aiding them. Mum is an example of an ordinary person who constantly demonstrates a commitment to kindness and determination to help others. When the civil war ended, my mother sponsored several children from her village and sent them to schools in Aweil town. In 2008 and 2012, she returned and provided clothes to numerous families. When famine was declared in 2013 in Northern Bahr el Ghazel, she supported families financially through those difficult times. When a member of a village is injured from landmines (explosive devices) while farming, she sends money to assist. In good or bad times, Mum demonstrates incredible compassion and dedication to helping others. This made her a worthy hero that the villagers truly admire.

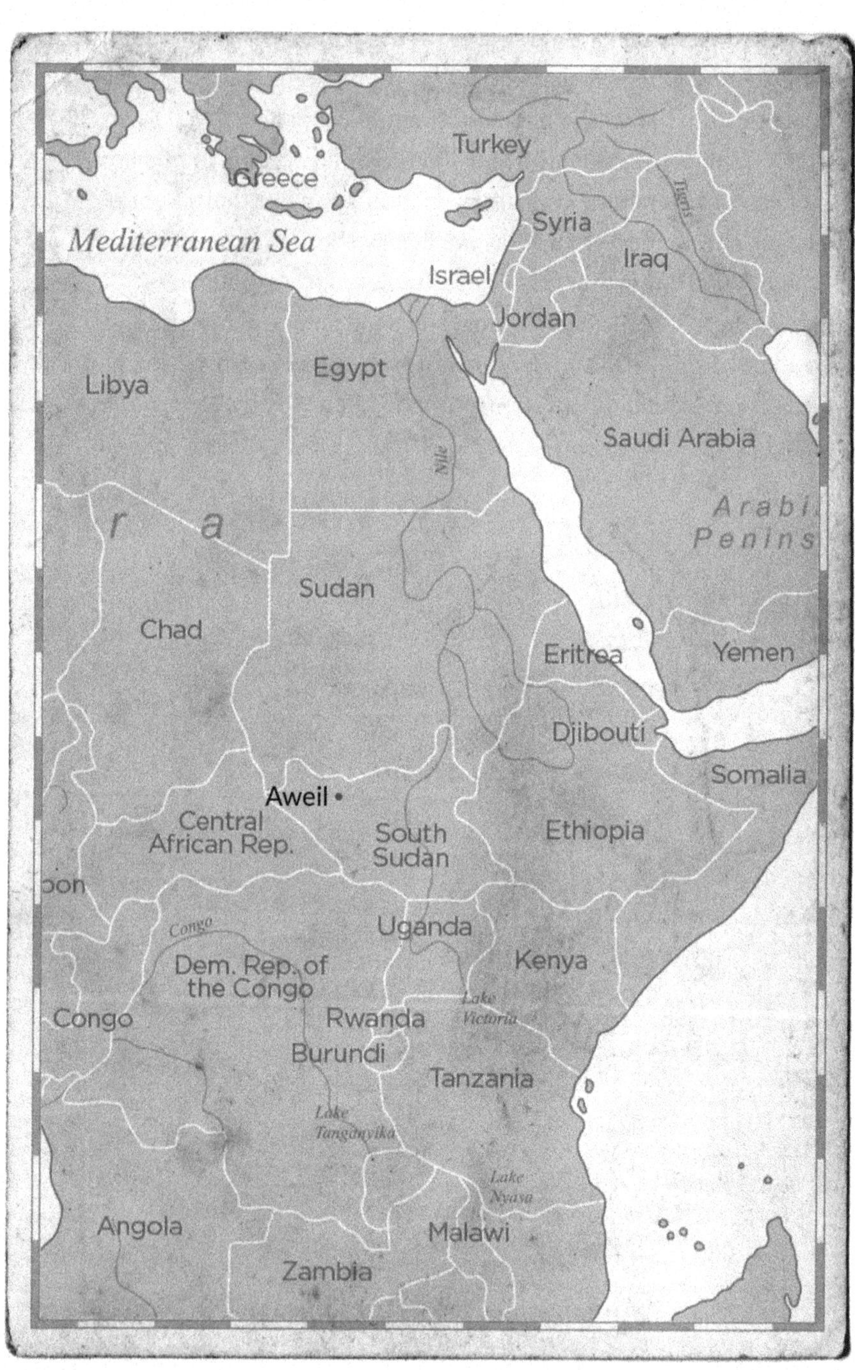

Greece
Turkey
Mediterranean Sea
Syria
Israel
Iraq
Tigris
Jordan
Libya
Egypt
Saudi Arabia
Arabian Peninsula
Nile
Sudan
Chad
Eritrea
Yemen
Djibouti
Somalia
Aweil
Central African Rep.
South Sudan
Ethiopia
Uganda
Congo
Kenya
Dem. Rep. of the Congo
Rwanda
Lake Victoria
Congo
Burundi
Tanzania
Lake Tanganyika
Lake Nyasa
Angola
Malawi
Zambia

CHAPTER 11

Family Reunion

**You have sorrow now, but I will see
you again, and your hearts will rejoice,
and no one will take your joy from you.**

– John 16:22 (NIV)

After living in displacement camps for more than fifteen years and several years as a refugee in Egypt, and then having lived in America for more than six years, my mother became more and more homesick for her village. She began to think about the possibility of reuniting with her mother and siblings if any of them were still alive. In 2005, the long and bloody Second Sudanese Civil War came to an end through the Comprehensive Peace Agreement signed by the Sudan People's Liberation Army (SPLA) and the Sudan government in Khartoum. This peace agreement brought relief and joy to my mother and the rest of the southern Sudanese community in the diaspora who had been forced out of their beloved home country for years due to the long-lasting civil war.

Later that year, my older sister Aketch called from Khartoum and told Mum that her mother and her siblings were still alive. My mother received this news with great joy, and she could not wait to reunite with her family whom she loved and missed dearly. Since the moment she received the good news, my mother planned to visit the new Republic of South Sudan. On more than one occasion she tried to make travel plans, but certain things out of her control kept preventing her. The country was still not stable, and my stepfather was often admitted to the hospital in North Carolina.

We were still in school, and Mum had to work to pay bills and provide for the family, so traveling for Mum was complicated. She could not save enough money for the cost of travel. All these issues that kept coming up pushed her travel plans back even further. My mother realized the longer she waited for the right time to come, the further away she was from going home to see her family. At the end of 2007, my mother borrowed $2,000 from a family friend, plus the money she had saved up, to purchase a round-trip ticket to South Sudan.

This was her first trip back home since she fled her village over twenty-five years ago. It's often hard to believe what our mother sacrificed all those years for us to have a brighter future. When her village was burned down to ashes in 1983, it was my grandmother who advised my mother to run away with her children, to seek refuge somewhere safer, in any country beyond our borders. This was the last conversation Mum had with her mother all those years ago. Twenty-plus years later, Mum was successful in doing what her mother advised her years ago because she brought her children to the greatest country on the face of the Earth, the United States.

Finally, in 2008, my mother traveled from the United States to Aweil, South Sudan. My mother was very excited to go to South Sudan to visit her mother and siblings. I cannot even describe how joyful she was. Days before she was set to fly from Charlotte to Washington Dulles International Airport to Addis Ababa Bole International, she said, "I am very excited to visit because it's been a long time, and I never thought this day would come. At the same time, I am so anxious to see my family, especially my mother. I wonder how old my mother is now." When my family arrived in the United

States in March 2001, we had never been on an airplane before, and
that experience was incredible. My mother got on an airplane for the
second time in her life to visit a village on the other side of the world,
a place called Panjab.

After nearly twelve hours of flying over the mighty Atlantic Ocean,
she landed in Addis Ababa, Ethiopia. In Ethiopia, she rested and
refreshed herself after a long flight. The next day she took another
plane for Juba, the capital of South Sudan. After two hours in flight,
my mother reached Juba. Twenty-five years ago, Juba International
Airport was nothing but a battle zone between the Sudan People's
Liberation Army (SPLA), a rebel army that was fighting for freedom
of southern Sudan, and the predominately Arab armed forces from
northern Sudan. My sister Aketch and her family had recently moved
back to South Sudan directly from the displacement camp, feeling
it was safe after the peace agreement was signed. Aketch waited
impatiently for Mum at the gate, excited to see her mother for the
first time since we left for Egypt in 1997. A minute later, she spotted
Mum as she recognized the cloth my mother wore that day. The two
spotted each other from across the waiting area, and then my sister
ran full speed into a huge embrace. She was all over Mum as they
embraced each other, and the tears of joy slowly poured. "There
is nothing like being reunited with your daughter after being away
from her for a long time," said my mother. The moment was special,
and it involved an epic slow-motion-worthy moment where love and
affection took the show. People around them were confused about
what was going on, but my sister later told a few people in the waiting
area, "My mother has returned home."

After this epic moment at the airport, my mother and sister were
on their way to Aweil. After an hour and half by air, they made it to
Aweil. Once they arrived, they took a taxi to Panjab. In Panjab, my
grandmother, aunts, uncles, and other relatives were waiting for her
arrival. After a long ride over bumpy, unpaved roads from the Aweil
airport to the village, my mother and sister finally made it to Panjab.
As the taxi began to turn toward a grass-thatched mud hut, an elderly

lady accompanied by a group of people stepped out of the house. The vehicle stopped, and my mother and sister started to walk toward the house as the taxi driver assisted with unloading Mum's bags. The eighty-five-year-old elderly woman immediately recognized her daughter, even though she had not seen her in decades. While Mum was still a long way off, her mother saw her and was filled with love for her. Grandma Abuk took off at full speed and threw her arms around her daughter and kissed her.

"Almighty God, you are great! You brought my child back!" said Grandma Abuk. "Oh God, my daughter is alive! I have been asking about you my whole life." They both began to cry. Tears of joy poured down their faces as they embraced. My mother's siblings joined in, and then everybody was crying and joyful.

"Adout, we thought you were dead a long time ago," said one of my aunts.

"I am so happy to get my child back alive. All the words I can say and more praises to the Almighty God. I could not stop thinking about her. I thought about her every day of my life, and I asked God not to take me away before I can see my baby again," said Grandma Abuk.

"Mum, I am here, and I have never forgotten about you," my mother told Grandma Abuk. "It came in my dream. I had dreamed that this is the way it would happen, and when it did, it was all God's plan for us, reunited again in peace."

"How are the children doing?" Grandma Abuk asked.

"They are all well and safe in America. They are all grown up. I brought their photos for all of you to see," my Mum replied.

Once inside, Grandma Abuk said, "Come and sit on my lap, my child."

My mother refused. "I can't, Mum. I am a grown woman now." Mum and her siblings laughed.

"I don't care how old you are. You are still my child regardless of your age," said Grandma in a motherly voice that showed love and affection. My grandma's offer to have my mother sit on her lap may seem silly, but Grandma's unconditional love toward her child called for such a move. It's unbelievable that an eighty-five-year-old mother would still remind her fifty-one-year-old daughter that she was still her baby regardless of age. It's true that there is no stronger love in this world than the love a mother feels for her child.

Nearly twenty-five years from the day Mum fled into the bush for safety as her village burned, mother and daughter met again in the small village where they once lived peacefully before the Second Sudanese Civil War. My mother had reunited with her long-lost family, especially her mother whom she never stopped loving or missing. As Grandma and Mum tried to make up for their lost years, Grandma knew that Mum made the right decision when she ran away with the children to take them away from civil war. When my mother sat next to Grandma to show her pictures of us, Grandma congratulated her because she was very happy for her daughter. Grandma Abuk said, "I am happy for you because you have daughters and sons of your own. The girls are beautiful, and the boys are handsome and strong. You made a right decision at the time of war—I know you did. It takes a woman with a heart of gold and bravery to do what you did." On the second day of her stay in Panjab, more and more of Mum's relatives came from far distances on foot to meet her. My uncles and other relatives, as is tradition, brought a cow to be slaughtered to celebrate my mother's return home. They began to celebrate with happiness and smiles. It was a remarkable experience and epic moment for Mum and her family.

On April 5, 2016, I traveled to South Sudan to visit my mother's village for the first time. I had never been to South Sudan before as I was born in the displacement camp in the north when Sudan was still one country. My siblings and I learned about Panjab through stories Mum shared with us when we were young. The only person I knew when I arrived in Aweil, South Sudan, was my older sister Aketch Maywal. She survived the brutal Sudanese war with her family and moved back to South Sudan after the hard-won independence on July 9, 2011. My sister and I were split apart when Mum and the rest of the family fled the civil war all those years ago. When my sister and I met at Aweil airstrip on April 6, it was an emotional reunion, and tears of joy ran down our faces. It was an unbelievable moment as none of us thought we would meet again. The last time she saw me, I was a young boy, and now I'm a grown man.

I stayed at my sister's house in Aweil town for a couple of days. On April 8, my sister took me to my mother's village to meet with other family members. A gentleman who was a friend to the family had a car. He volunteered to give us a ride to the village, which was forty minutes from the town. When I arrived in Panjab, I received a traditional blessing from my uncle, who was the chief of the village. He poured splashes of water on my feet and sprayed my body with water. He called upon our ancestral spirits to thank them and asked them to watch over me while I was in the country and when I returned to the US. My uncles and the community members sacrificed a cow to celebrate my visit to the village. Women from the community sang songs and danced to celebrate and welcome me. Once the food was ready, we ate the delicious dish under a huge tree in cool shade. While we were enjoying ourselves, we had to fight off flies and wild falcons that flew over our heads in a circle as they tried to snatch away the food from our hands. I must admit that one must have a strong stomach and courage to eat at all in such a situation.

While I was in Panjab, my uncles took the time to show me around. They took me to see the site where the first chief of the village, my grandfather, was buried. I paid my respects silently to the chief, and I was moved by the legacy my grandfather left behind for his people. In 2012 when Mum returned to South Sudan for a second time, she hired people to build a tomb on the site where her father was laid to rest. She wanted everyone to know where he was buried. I saw a huge tree called Quel that my grandfather had once sat under to peacefully solve disputes among the community. My aunt's husband took me to Machar where I saw the large land that Grandpa used to farm and provide for his family. I was stunned to see the water well that my grandfather dug with his own bare hands and drank from. I saw trees where Grandpa once cut to build a house next to his farm.

Also, I was able to pay my respects to Grandma, who is buried at my aunt's house. There, I also saw an unmarked site where three of my mother's children were buried and stood at the piece of land that was once the site of my mother's first house as a young woman.

While in South Sudan, I was able to meet my mother's younger brother, Ungua, her only full sibling still living. When Mum's village was burned down to ashes in 1983, this uncle was forced to be a child soldier. He was thirteen when he was conscripted to the Sudan People's Liberation Army (SPLA), the guerrilla freedom fighters that battled the oppressive regime based in Khartoum. When I met my uncle, he was a stranger to me, just as I was to him. Through the stories Mum had told us, I had heard about him, but I never thought I would get to meet him in person.

When he arrived, I was in the middle of a conversation with other family members. Then suddenly my sister told me, "Bol, this is Uncle Ungua, Mum's brother." I respectfully got up to shake his hand and hug him. The clothes he wore were dirty, smelly, and ripped apart. He had on a dirty, torn orange cap. I took it off his head and replaced it with my brand new Under Armour cap that I bought a week before in the US. It did not matter to me what he had on or how bad he smelled. He was my hero, the man who influenced me to become a professional soldier. We went to a nearby market to buy him clothes in addition to my own clothes that I had given him. Uncle Ungua is someone I was glad to get to know personally. He was someone I respected and admired as a liberator and a warrior, and I thanked him for his service.

I never shared with my uncle and other family members that I was a soldier. As someone who is a professional soldier and a member of the best army that ever existed in the history of humankind, I respect my Uncle Ungua, who was once a child rebel and soldier who helped liberate his country to achieve independence. It felt surreal to meet him in person and actually get to know him. My uncle was a small guy, about five feet, seven inches tall, and weighed about 115 pounds. I could look deep into his eyes and soul and see that he was a good person. He was a father to his children, a husband to his wife, and a brother to his sisters. He had a laid-back personality blended with confidence and a sense of humor. Like many guerrilla fighters who have been neglected, my uncle returned to his father's village after the war ended in 2005 to battle post-traumatic stress disorder (PTSD) on his own and in extreme poverty. This is the dark side of war, and his invisible wounds spilled over to peace time.

I was aware that my uncle had PTSD, and I tried to avoid discussing anything that traumatized him. Sometimes he voluntarily told interesting facts about his days in the bush during the liberation struggle. "SPLA gave me an education and an AK-47. I learned how to count in English in Ethiopia," he proudly said with a friendly smile on his face. "Bol, if you look over there, I guarantee you that you will find my bullet shells from the days of liberation. I remember vividly how we defended Aweil from a determined enemy that attempted to recapture it. We fought tooth and nail, and the SPLA won the battle." My uncle told me that he and his soldiers were made invincible to bullets through the help of a spiritual leader (a practitioner of traditional African religion) who had spiritual powers that made them bulletproof to enemy fires. The spiritual leader gave them a medicine that shielded him. When he and his fellow soldiers first got the medicine from the spiritual leader, they would individually test it to make sure it worked. During the test, a fellow soldier volunteered to test the bulletproof medicine using his AK-47 rifle to shoot at each of them individually. Uncle Ungua and others were shot at one by one, and the bullets never landed on them. This "proved" that the supernatural medicine worked, and they went on to survive battle after battle until South Sudan was liberated.

Life in South Sudan and our life in America are incomparable. My siblings and I are very fortunate to have grown up in the United States. The village of Panjab where my Mum grew up was frozen in time. For more than seventy years, the village has been without proper development due to colonialism under British rule and decades of civil wars. The majority of people there, including my family members, live in absolute poverty. While I was in Panjab village, sleeping outside under the stars, I would reflect on the things my Mother once shared about her village. During my brief time there, I was able to witness the resilience of the people in Panjab and across South Sudan. In Panjab specifically, there is no electricity to bring these poor villagers out of the darkness. There are no hospitals or clinics to heal the curable diseases that often plague them. There is no clean, running water for drinking or bathing. Folks still use ancient water wells and water pumps to get water. There is no proper school for children to attend. There is no infrastructure such as roads or decent housing. People still live in their mud hut houses and sleep on blankets on the floor. The only semblance of infrastructure I saw was an eroded road and a poorly maintained train track built by the British during the colonial era.

Independence on July 9, 2011, did not bring peace to South Sudan as expected. On December 15, 2013, soldiers loyal to President Salva Kiir and soldiers loyal to Vice President Riek Machar, PhD, fired shots at each other at the presidential palace in Juba triggering additional conflict. It started as a result of a power struggle between Kiir, a Dinka, and Machar, a Nuer. During the following week, the fighting escalated quickly and spread to three strategic states: Jongeli, Unity, and Upper Nile. The violent conflict took on an ethnic dimension between the country's largest ethnic groups, the Dinka and the Nuer (Rolandsen 2015). Approximately 400,000 were reported to have been killed and hundreds of thousands displaced from their homes. The country quickly descended into a violent conflict only two years after it gained its hard-won independence from Sudan. Once again, the aspirations of the people of South Sudan were threatened by another war that reached its fifth year.

My visit to South Sudan in 2016 was a risk that I took out of desperation to see family members who survived conflict for more than twenty-two years. When I arrived in South Sudan, I registered at the US embassy in Juba since I was an American citizen. In case of an emergency, Americans citizens inside the country would be evacuated and taken to a neighboring country. During my short visit, I was not able to meet all the family members due to time constraints and the fact that everybody was spread out. It was impossible to travel around every three days to visit each family because roads were so bad and phone communication very limited. My male cousins, nephews, and other male relatives were dragged to the front line and fought on the South Sudan government's side in the current war. While I was in the country, I avoided political conversations. I focused my time and energy on having a great time with family and prayed that I would return safely to the US. To those who were not family members, I was just another foreigner in South Sudan. While I am relatively tall and fit and have smooth, black skin, I did not look South Sudanese enough to them. To my sister, the only person I knew in South Sudan, I was her little brother who had returned to his ancestral home after years abroad.

While there, I enjoyed spending time with my nephews and nieces, and I went to collect water at the water pump with my nieces. Typically, the role of water collection is assigned to girls and women in patriarchal society. I did not mind, and I wanted to help out while putting smiles on the faces of my nieces. In addition, I had a lot of fun with my nephews. They played with their simple toy—a tire from a motorbike. When I told them that I used to play with a similar one when I was a boy at the refugee camp, they did not believe me. So I took the tire and showed them how it was done; they were all amazed. In the morning, I walked my nieces and nephews to school. At noon, I went to each of their schools to collect them and walk them back home. They loved my company, and I learned so much from them. When they discovered that I was scheduled to return to America in a week, they asked me if they could come to America with me. I told them that South Sudan has potential to be like America in terms of peace, justice, equality, and prosperity. It's all a matter of time before these things become a reality.

While I was in South Sudan, I took a lot of pictures to capture every moment to the best of my ability. I recorded greetings on my camera from our South Sudanese family there to our family in America. I photographed places such as Grandpa's tomb, farms, land, and my Mum's first home to show my American siblings. I recorded Aunty Achan's home where my Grandma is laid to rest. Basically, I recorded pieces of family history that will be beneficial not only to my siblings but also to my American-born nieces and nephews, who have no knowledge of their ancestral home in South Sudan. The photos I took while in South Sudan should be a constant reminder of how fortunate we are to have come to America. My family has come a long way, and Mum sacrificed so much to reach the shores of freedom in America.

When I left Aweil, it was a very emotional moment for my sister and me. It was hard for her to let her little brother go, but I promised her and the family that I would return again one day. So far, I am the only child among my siblings in America to have returned to war-torn South Sudan in a quest to reunite with family members. My brief time in South Sudan was a trip to remember, and it was worth the risk to me. While there, I discovered that South Sudan was as wealthy in natural resources as the village my grandfather founded, and from that moment, I knew brighter days were ahead!

Left to right: Aunty Achan, Aketch Maywal (sister), Akol (niece), and Bol in Panjab circa 2016. *Photo courtesy of Nygan Wek.*

Uncle Ungua

Adout's mother, Abuk Makuach, is buried according to Luo tradition and custom at the family residence at Achan's house. *Photo courtesy of Maywal Maywal.*

Left to right: deputy village chief, Aketch Maywal, Ungua Yot, Chief Lual Goi Ungua (Adout's half-brother), Lual Obour, and Bol holding his niece Akol paying respects in April 2016 to Bol's grandfather and founder of Panjab village. *Photo courtesy of Moses Goi.*

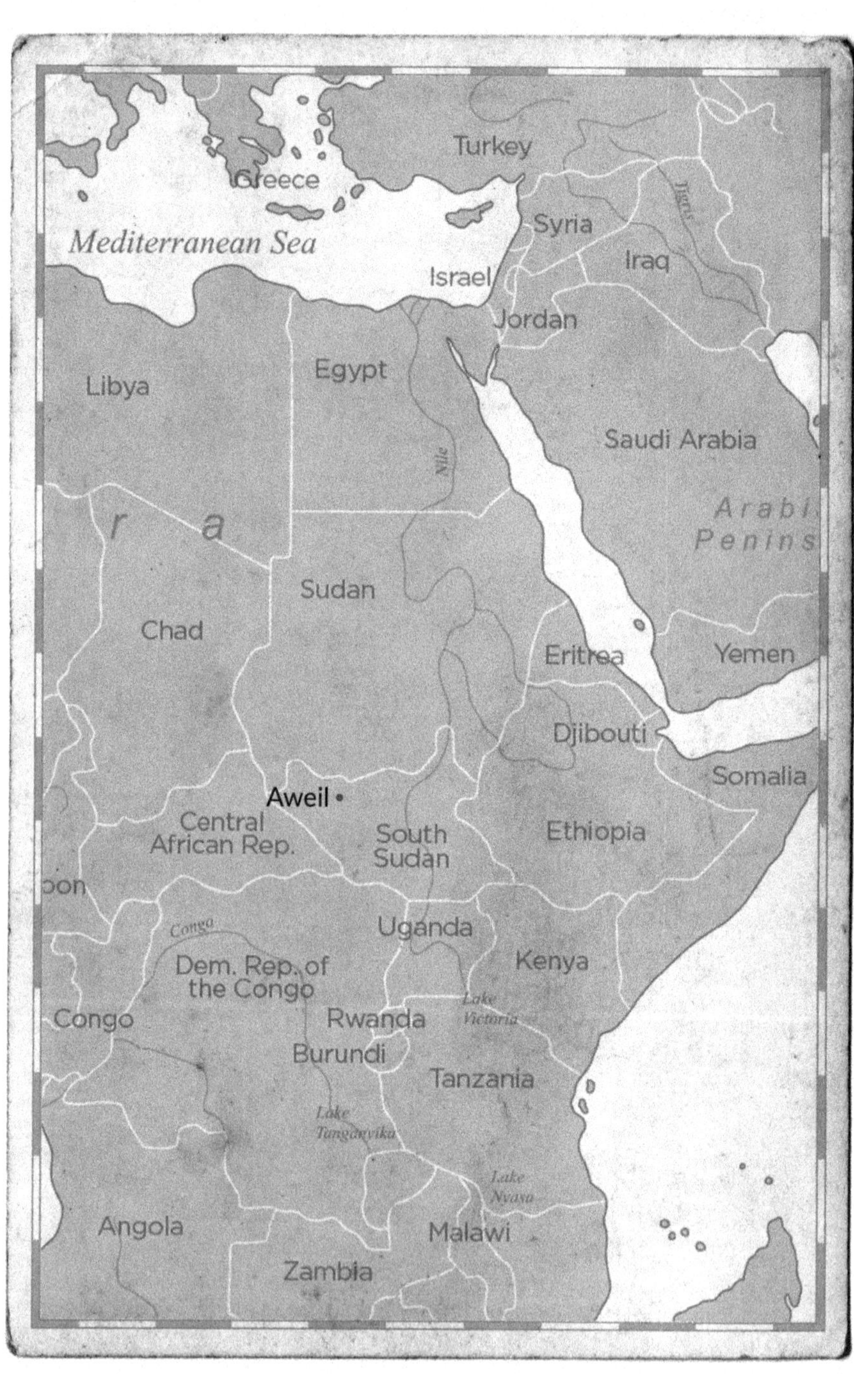

Greece
Turkey
Syria
Iraq
Israel
Jordan
Mediterranean Sea
Libya
Egypt
Saudi Arabia
Nile
Arabia
Penins
Sudan
Chad
Eritrea
Yemen
Djibouti
Aweil
Somalia
Central
African Rep.
South
Sudan
Ethiopia
Uganda
Congo
Kenya
Dem. Rep. of
the Congo
Rwanda
Lake
Victoria
Congo
Burundi
Tanzania
Lake
Tanganyika
Lake
Nyasa
Angola
Malawi
Zambia

The Father Who Wasn't

**It is a wise father that
knows his own child.**

– William Shakespeare,
The Merchant of Venice

I never really knew my biological father. The man who planted his seed into my mother's womb was never part of my life. My siblings and I were raised by Mum and my stepfather, James Nagan. My siblings and I grew up knowing that James Nagan was only the biological father of my two younger brothers, Amoe and Makot.

In Luo tradition, my father was Uchu Maywal, the man who paid my mother's dowry and married her when she was a young woman. Uchu Maywal was killed in southern Sudan during the civil war, and I've always felt it was an honor to be given his name. Again in Luo tradition, a man's brother or cousin can step in to take care of his widow and her children. This practice preserves the family name, blood line, and legacy. When Uchu Maywal passed away, one of his male relatives, Akol Dagon, was encouraged to take responsibility for the family. Though I did not meet him or even know about him until much later, Akol Dagon was my biological father.

When I was nineteen years old, I first started to get some hint that I had another "father" apart from my traditional father and stepfather. I heard Mum make jokes about where I got my skin tone, hair, eyes, height, walk, and the whole good looks. We laughed whenever she teased me this way. It was not taken seriously because I never knew another man besides my stepfather, James Nagan. I guess to her, it might have been the right time to reveal the truth when I realized that it was our Luo culture and custom to ignore my biological father. My mother had done nothing wrong, nor did she attempt to hide anything from me. She was just following our Luo cultural practice. But she felt comfortable talking about my biological father with me when I reached an appropriate age.

In 2013, my mother made a phone call to Aweil, South Sudan, to check on Aketch and her family. While she was on the phone, Mum got the news that my biological father, Akol, was at Aketch's house. When Mum spoke to my sister about his condition, Mum learned that Akol had been very sick and had left his wife due to some domestic issues between them. Akol had lost a lot of weight since his wife refused to look after him—she only cooked enough for herself and the kids. Constant arguments between Akol and his wife led to fights that seemed unending. He eventually left his wife because she was not taking care of him, especially when he was ill and needed support the most. He went to Aketch's place because he had nobody else to go to for help. I was in my room when Mum was on the phone with my sister, ignorant of who my biological father was at that point.

Mum asked me to speak on the phone, and I thought I would be speaking to my sister. But I spoke to a stranger who I learned that night was my biological father. I was twenty-three years old when I spoke to Akol Dagon for the first time in my life, at least that I remembered. "Hello, how are you guys doing?" I said thinking I was on the phone with my sister. A man replied in Luo dialect, but I could not comprehend what exactly he was saying. So I politely switched to Dinka dialect and asked, "Who am I speaking with?" since I could not recognize the voice.

My mother kindly took the phone away from my hand and told the
man that my Luo dialect was limited and that he needed to speak to
me in Dinka. Mum then told me that it was Akol Dagon on the phone
and that I should speak in Dinka with him. We were both comfortable
speaking Dinka, so we spoke for about two minutes, but I had no idea
what to talk about since he was a stranger to me. I asked him how he
was doing and wished him a quick recovery. I told him that he would
be fine and not to lose hope because there was a cure for whatever
he had. I learned that while he was out farming, a large branch from a
tree had fallen on his left shoulder.

I knew nothing about the man who called me "my son" that night
as I spoke to him on the phone. Traditionally, my biological father had
no right to claim me as his child. Mum told me he was a nice guy on
all accounts, a very handsome man, good with kids, and he took good
care of my older siblings before I came along. She painted a picture of
him as peaceful, fun loving, and a great dancer of *adhu*, our Luo dance.
She also said he loved his family and relatives and kept them near
his heart. He never spanked any of my siblings, but rather used his
sense of humor and other tactics to get the kids to listen to him. Mum
admired these things about Akol Dagan, and while they were together,
Mum believed him to be an honest man, which she respected greatly.

Much later, I learned the exact circumstances of my conception.
My parents never planned to have me; my biological father had
forced himself on my mother. This revelation shocked me and left
me speechless. She later discovered that she was pregnant with me.
If this were to happen today, he would be held accountable for his
act in prison. Unfortunately, this took place many years ago in Sudan,
and my father walked free for two reasons. First, Mum kept silent,
probably because nobody would have believed her. Second, Akol was
already considered a family member and traditional ways shielded him
from punishment. After knowing this sad truth, the only thing I could
do is to do what I have been doing since I was a teenager: keep "some
filial token to repay her brave and tender love," as Louisa May Alcott
beautifully put it.

Akol drank heavily, which caused problems. Whenever he was drunk, he would start arguments with my mother. He would also get into fights with my uncles who lived nearby. She said the alcohol in his system caused him to get into a lot of trouble, but when he was not intoxicated, Mum says he was a nice person and a great father.

He could not find a job in the displacement camp. It was easy for women to work for Arabs as domestic servants, but it was generally difficult for men to find jobs. My biological father lacked many skills, including speaking Arabic. He was a farmer before the war broke out in southern Sudan. According to my mother, Akol never bothered to go out and find a job to support the family. He would rather iron the few clothes he had and step out to go wherever alcohol was served, and then he would come back home drunk. Education was another thing Akol did not have, but Mum could not blame him for this because the vast majority of southern Sudanese people did not have this opportunity. Lack of leadership was another element that Mum did not like; he was more of a follower than a leader, from Mum's perspective. He was not a man of his own ideas because his actions were based off what others told him. The fact that he listened to others and did not think for himself was problematic.

It was painful for me to learn that my biological father left Mum when I was near death as a toddler and never bothered to come see me or ask of me the entire time I was in Sudan. My family escaped to Egypt and stayed there as refugees for two years, and he never cared to check on the family. It's difficult for me to imagine that my biological father would leave his own flesh and blood and walk away just because of the harsh conditions in Sudan. Giving up and walking away was the easy path out of responsibility for him. Aside from my illness, there might have been other factors that drove him away. It's true that life in the displacement camps was not easy, but that should not serve as an excuse to walk away and never come back. Shortly after Akol Dagan left the family, James Nagan came into our lives. Unlike my biological father, my stepfather had an opportunity to go to school in his teenage years in Khartoum because he had left southern Sudan earlier.

When Mum visited South Sudan in 2008, we missed her terribly for the two months she was away from us. We were used to having our mom around, and we were happy when she returned to the States safe and sound. She visited another world that looked unfamiliar to her after twenty-five years of not seeing her mother and her other siblings who were still alive when she escaped in 1983. She shared her brief experience about this fragile southern region of Sudan that was on its way to becoming an independent country. Some of the stories she shared with us brought back old memories about how terrible life was in Sudan under harsh conditions of hunger, thirst, and life-claiming diseases. Her stories also reminded us that we were indeed blessed to reach the shores of freedom here in the West, but at the same time, the hardships that our relatives were facing back home was constantly on our minds. Mum brought a message to share with us. She told us that the family extended their greetings and were happy to have photos of us that Mum took with her.

My grandmother remembered Aketch and Allah-jabo because they were the children Mum escaped with when her village was burned down to ashes by government aircraft. My other siblings and I were born in the displacement camps around Sudan. All of our relatives and her family were happy that Mum visited them, and they did not believe their eyes that she was really back. They thought she was dead a long time ago. Since the majority of my family members had never met us, Mum told them about us and showed them the photos she brought with her. Mum told us that she sat down with an album on her lap, and everybody made a circle around her in order to see our pictures. She would flip through the pictures and tell them who they were looking at.

Mum told us that of all the pictures in the album, my photo took the show, and everybody wanted to have one for themselves. The fact that my photo was the most admired got me wondering, so I asked Mum to explain why everybody wanted photos of me. "It was not all the photos of you that they wanted. The picture of you wearing your military uniform was the one they loved," she told me. Then I remembered the picture from high school where I wore my Army green class A uniform with my grey beret and my cadet rank pin on it. I wore a red cord on my right shoulder for being a member of the drill team, and I had a shining drill tab that I earned from drill team competition in high school. I also wore a green cord on my left shoulder because I was among the senior leadership in the JROTC program at Myers Park.

My military bearing was clear in the picture they liked, and I looked sharp, handsome, and powerful to them. In that photo I had the image of a leader in the making, and the picture itself displayed the discipline of the US Army. "He looks like a commander in the US Army," one of my relatives said to Mum. She laughed and then told them, "No, Bol is in the JROTC in high school, and he is not officially in the military yet. He wants to continue."

The US Army is well respected around the world, and for my poor family in the forgotten part of the world to see their own relative in the uniform made them proud of me. Hence, my picture in the JROTC uniform was put up nicely inside their mud house walls in South Sudan. Mum told us about the message that our family wanted us to never forget. She told all of us the family wanted to send this message to us: "Don't forget about us because being family is in blood, and distance cannot separate us. We will meet again in the name of the Almighty God. Let the children in the USA focus on getting their education because education is power."

My biological father, Akol Dagon, was among the family members who managed to get a picture of me. He heard from another relative who had spread the news about Mum's presence in Aweil, South Sudan, to visit her ill mother and the rest of the family. When my biological father took a good look at my picture with me in my US Army uniform, he saw a mirror image of himself. He was shaken to see a picture of his own flesh that he abandoned twenty years ago. The last time he saw me was when I was a sickly toddler, yet he chose to walk away from my mother's life with me battling chicken pox and acute malnutrition, which threatened the lives of thousands of newborns in the displacement camps. With news of my mother in town, Akol saw a different picture of me. He saw a kid that was once on his way to death back in those difficult days in the displacement camp now in a uniform looking sharp and resurrected, something he never imagined. He saw not just a reflection of himself in the picture, but also a leader in the making. He saw the hard work of a woman behind the teen in uniform and felt speechless. When Mum shared this with me, I did not have anything to say and only thanked God for giving us such an amazing mother.

After I graduated from college in 2013, I had planned to visit South Sudan and meet my father. I was interested to hear his version of the story about why he left the family, especially when I was ill. I wanted to be fair to him and hear what he had to say. Unfortunately, my plan to visit was delayed due to conflict that erupted in South Sudan in December 2013. From information I gathered from my mother and older sister, I concluded that my biological dad was not a bad guy after all. My older siblings admired him and praised the father he was to them when he was with the family. I have never heard anything negative about him from my siblings, nor did I ever hear anything negative from people who knew him. My mother never felt any animosity toward him. When he was reported sick in 2013, my mother asked me to send money to him, but I refused because I was angry with him for not being there for me. Later, I changed my mind and sent the money. In addition, my mother sent my father money for him to support his family.

On April 11, 2015, I woke up to the news that my biological father had passed from the injury he sustained when the tree branch fell between his neck and left shoulder two years earlier. The injury never truly healed and led to chronic pain and swelling. His relatives attempted to take him to the nearest clinic possible, but the pain was too much to bear. To make the situation worse, transportation was difficult to find from the village of Barmayen (where he lived) to

Aweil where there was a clinic. Unfortunately, his relatives tried to ease the pain through a traditional way, which required a cut to the tip of the swollen area. One relative made the cut in order to release the built-up fluid around his neck, which resulted in internal bleeding and infection that led to his death. My mother received a phone call that morning, and I did not know how I should feel because he was still a stranger to me. I felt compassion because what happened was horrible to say the least. I was looking forward to meeting him when I travel to South Sudan, but I knew that he belonged to the ages. I was left with nothing but to forgive him.

I discovered that I have a half-brother and a half-sister in South Sudan. Their names are Akon, a girl, and Unguec, a boy. They have lived with their uncle in Barmayen village in Aweil since their mother passed. Unfortunately, their mother died shortly after my biological father passed. This circumstance left Akol's brother to look after the children. While I was in the country, I never had the opportunity to meet up with them due to time and distance constraints. Before Akol passed, he asked Aketch to look after the children. Traditionally, the children cannot join our family without my family paying money in exchange for the children. This is absolutely ridiculous, and it complicates things. My sister had requested the children join her in Aweil, so they could go to school, but their uncle refused. I often wonder if my half-siblings know of me. I like to assume that Akol told them, but I won't know until I find out myself. Next time I visit South Sudan, I will do my best to go look after them and have DNA tests done to make sure they are truly my siblings.

I am thankful for the time my biological father was there for my siblings. I knew him only through the words of others, and I pray his precious soul rests easy in heaven. We did not have the chance to meet here on Earth, but we shall meet in heaven. I have learned many things because of the absence of my biological father in my life. One day, I want to be a great father to my own children and be there for them to give them my love and affection. I knew my father was not a leader, so this is part of the reason I am determined to be a good leader. I knew my father and mother did not have education, so I have taken my education seriously. My father was an alcoholic, so I chose to never drink alcohol in my life. My mother has instilled in me a deep sense of obligation to one day be a great father in the best way I can be to my future children. Mum was both a father and a mother in all the ways any child can ever wish for. She is the angel that lightens our world, and God is the father who guided our path in life.

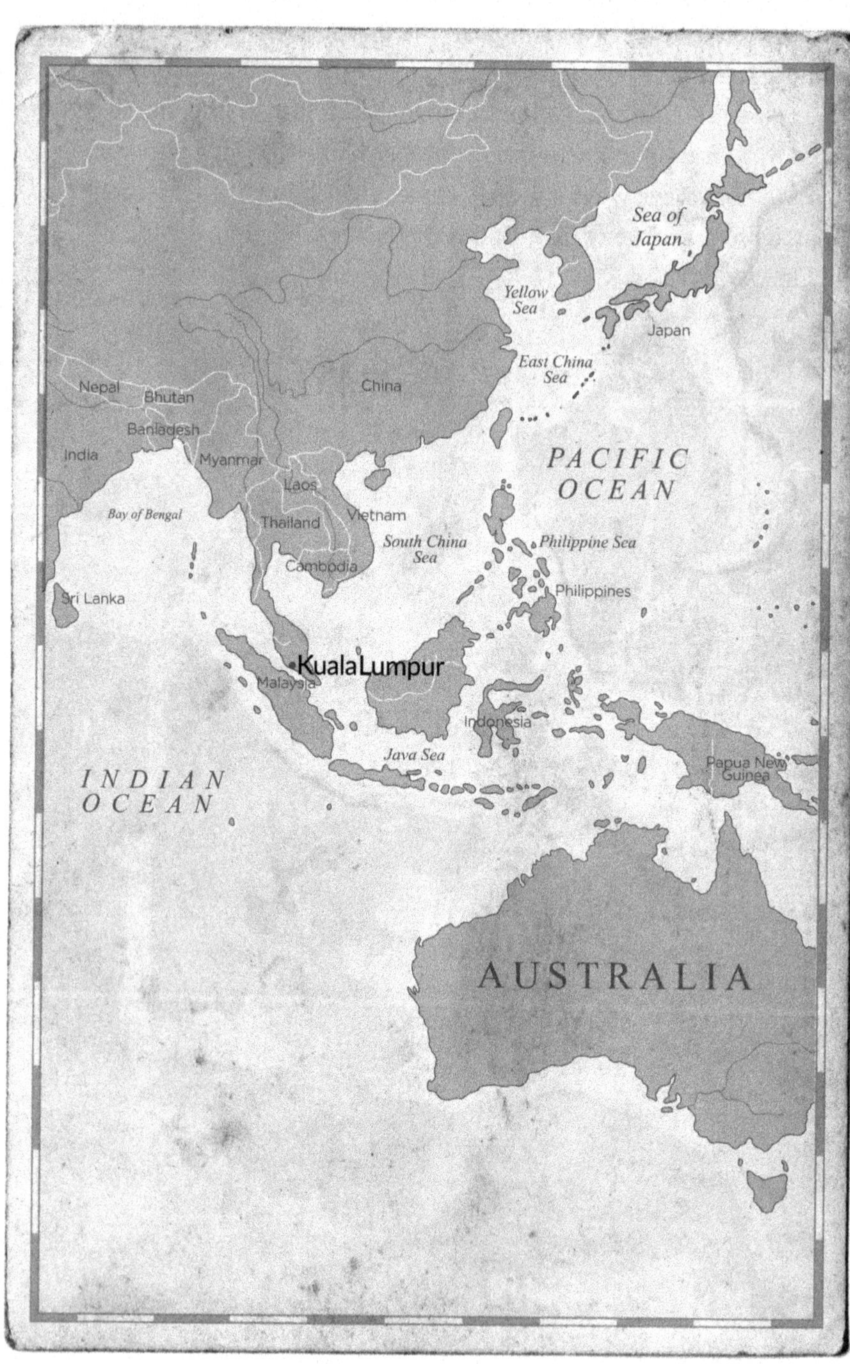

Sea of Japan
Yellow Sea
Japan
East China Sea
Nepal
Bhutan
Banladesh
India
Myanmar
China
PACIFIC OCEAN
Laos
Bay of Bengal
Thailand
Vietnam
Cambodia
South China Sea
Philippine Sea
Philippines
Sri Lanka
Kuala Lumpur
Malaysia
Indonesia
Java Sea
Papua New Guinea
INDIAN OCEAN
AUSTRALIA

CHAPTER 13

Love and Romance

**A man without a wife is like
a vase without flowers.**

– African Proverb

When it comes to relationships and choosing future partners, my mother had high expectations for all of us. For her five boys whom she raised to become men and two beautiful girls to become women, we were held to the same high standard. Because she is the eldest surviving sibling, Aketch was the first to get married according to our Luo culture. She married a Dinka gentleman in the 1990s while we were still in Sudan. When we arrived in the US, Mum wanted all of us to pursue education and dreams before deciding to get married.

Growing up in America, I heard people say that marriage is not necessary, and it seems not as cherished as it once was. A century ago, there was no question whether marriage was necessary or not because it was part of life, and everyone knew that they were products of their parents' love. From my observation of American culture, some people view marriage as nonessential, and others cherish it and advocate for it. The divorce rate in America is

50 percent, and that scares people and discourages some young people from properly marrying. Instead, many young people nowadays are starting families before getting married, and this is happening at an alarming rate.

When we reached our teenage years in America, Mum made it clear to all of us that marriage was a must. Everybody must marry, and it must be done in a right way, whether it was in our Luo traditional way or the American way. The choice was totally ours, and we were expected to bring partners that were exceptional. In my mother's generation, marriage was arranged or forced, and Mum knew that from her first-hand experience. Mum was forced to marry our father, Uchu Maywal, against her will, and she would not allow that to happen to any of her children in this modern age. In a way, we are lucky to have a mother who understood the consequences of forced marriage. Amal, Mum's only daughter in America, was free to choose the man of her dreams once she completed her education, an opportunity Mum never had growing up in southern Sudan.

Unfortunately, Amal fell short of Mum's expectations when she got pregnant during her junior year of high school. A Dinka man named Lual who had befriended our family took advantage of Amal's innocence. He was twenty-six years old, and she was seventeen, but she thought he cared for her. Mum was blown away and could not wrap her head around this. She was confused and disappointed. My parents were not aware of any boyfriend that Amal had. She never introduced anybody to the family that our parents were aware of. In southern Sudanese culture, there is no such thing as boyfriend or girlfriend. Men who were interested were expected to marry and not date. In my sister's case, several guys known as "lost boys" came forward to ask for Amal's hand. However, Amal refused their official requests to the family. Most of these guys were keen to wait until she completed her education, including university.

In Luo culture, a certain marriage procedure must be followed to fix the circumstances of Amal's pregnancy. A man who impregnates a young woman without officially proposing must keep her as a wife, and her parents must demand a dowry. Although Lual was a Dinka and not a Luo, the traditional practices are similar, but he refused to pay the dowry and became fierce, violent, and disrespectful toward my family. His behavior left my sister confused and feeling unloved, even though she stayed with him. The man she thought loved her was not man enough to show respect toward her parents. The least my parents expected from Lual was respect, an apology, and a demonstration that he was man enough to take care of Amal and her child. Lual did not seem to care.

In 2004, Amal and Lual left North Carolina for Wisconsin and then moved on to North Dakota. She quickly discovered that Lual was an abusive alcoholic and found herself in a toxic relationship where she was emotionally, mentally, and physically beaten. The years she spent with Lual were a long nightmare. She was constantly hurt, lied to, deceived, cheated on, and misled by this monstrous man. She stayed in the relationship for years and had three more children with him hoping he would change, but Lual had no desire to change.

In 2016, Lual hit Amal while their eldest son, Wleing, was around. My nephew called the police, and Lual was handcuffed and taken to jail. He was only in jail for a few days but never came home. Amal later learned from a mutual friend that Lual flew to South Sudan immediately upon his release. He never said goodbye to his kids or my sister. Amal was finally free from all the pain Lual caused her, thanks to her courageous son who called the police. While Lual was in Aweil, South Sudan, Amal discovered that he had married two Dinka girls and paid the dowry for both of them. Amal did not bother feeling jealous and wished him the best. Since then, Amal continued to raise her children on her own while attending community college.

While Lual was still with Amal, he used to lie to folks in their community that he had paid the dowry to marry Amal. He never paid any dowry because he never valued her nor loved her. The fact that Lual was willing to pay the dowry for other women demonstrated that he valued them and wanted to make a point to my sister. In other words, Amal was not worthy enough to be his wife, yet he fathered four children with her. It is possible that Lual never valued Amal for the simple fact that she was from a different ethnic group. Therefore, she needed to be looked down upon and beaten down mentally, emotionally, and physically. If this were the case, then Lual must have hidden his tribalism mindset from Amal at the beginning.

Tribalism exists among South Sudanese people just like racism exists among fellow Americans. Tribalism is a strong belief that one ethnic group is superior to another, and people ought to be loyal to one's own ethnic or social group. This could explain why my sister was taken for granted. Another explanation could be that Lual was just not a good man, and his behavior may not have been motivated by any beliefs.

Like most women who have been through a horrible relationship, Amal had every reason to give up on her dream for true love. She did not get what she was worth with Lual, but she learned from that experience. She learned to love herself enough and to stand her ground to do what is best for herself and her children. And she did not give up on her dream for true love.

In 2017, a kind gentleman by the name of Ajang Akol was interested in her, but she turned him down. Traumatized by her past experience, she was not ready to enter into a relationship. Ajang made several attempts, and my sister continued to say no. After serious thoughts and prayers, she decided to give him a chance. She told him that if he was serious, then he must go through Mum and our family and officially propose according to our culture. The gentleman seized the opportunity and traveled to Charlotte from Grand Rapids, Michigan. He came with two other guys and met with Allah-jabo and me.

Ajang was willing to marry Amal and take all four children from her previous relationship as his own. It takes a man with certain character and boldness to be willing to do all this. He was eager to pay the dowry and desired to be part of our family. We accepted him. Amal is now married to Ajang Akol, who is from the Dinka Bor ethnic group and a fellow South Sudanese-American. Amal's husband is a great man who displays utmost respect to her and the rest of the family members. The couple gave birth to beautiful twin daughters in April 2018 and are happily married according to our South Sudanese traditions. They live in Grand Rapids, Michigan, with all of their children. True love does exist, and it is real. The key is to make it work with the right person who values you as much as you value them.

When it came to my brothers and me, Mum knew that one day her sons were going to fall in love, leave her, and tightly cleave to their wives. Mum always wanted us to treat women with respect and to be great husbands to our future wives. She also shared her wisdom about things we ought to look for in a girl: "When the time comes for you guys, you should look for respect, gentleness, thoughtfulness, inner beauty, selflessness, patience, faith, and joy." She would tell us this whenever we happened to be around at dinner time. These eight things to look for in a woman were drilled into our heads. Mum emphasized inner beauty because she did not want her sons to fall for outer beauty, which can fade as women age. According to Mum, inner beauty will always outshine and outlast her outward beauty. Therefore, she wanted us to look beyond a pretty face and seek a woman's heart.

"Guys, look for respect from your future partners," she would say. "Look for a woman who demonstrates respect to her parents and others. All men desire to be respected by their wives." Mum believes a woman who shows respect to others will know how to give something valuable to your relationship. Mum would go on and suggest that "with respect comes gentleness and patience." Mum believes that gentleness, respect, and patience must all go together. She believes gentleness and patience allow a woman to respond to frustration and conflict with grace, rather than unceasing anger that would escalate things in the event of a conflict between husband and wife.

Although looking for respect, honesty, gentleness, thoughtfulness, inner beauty, selflessness, patience, faith, and joy are good things to desire in a future partner, it's almost impossible to find all this in one woman. The Bible says, "He who finds a wife finds what is good and receives favor from the Lord" (Proverbs 18:22, NIV). In other words, finding the right partner is a gift from God.

Allah-jabo has not been lucky when it comes to finding the right person. Most of the women he dated thought he had money. When he used to run Professional Cab Company, he attracted more women than I have ever seen in my life. He was his own boss and looked the part—a suit, a tie, a nice watch, and two cell phones, one for personal use and the other for business only. He was always looking sharp, and that attracted women from all walks of life. Most of the women he dated never lasted six months. The reason was pretty clear: he had no money, and there was no love from the women who chased him. The family met several of his girlfriends, and most of the girls came to realize that our family does not have much. These women had a perception that Allah-jabo had money because he had a business, but what they saw never translated into reality. Our family had little, and we were humble enough to accept whoever was introduced to the family. The perception of having money was his biggest challenge to finding a woman who could be a potential wife.

I had a privilege that none of my brothers had as an adult. Shortly after I graduated from college and received my commission as an officer, Mum's friends overwhelmed her with recommendations about which girl in the community I should consider. Most of my mother's friends recommended their own daughters who were my age for future partners. Most of these suggestions were brought to my attention, but others were kept a secret for the fear that I would turn them down. Similarly, friends of my sisters made suggestions. Although recommendations are considered an honor, I never wanted my future partner to be found for me. I always wanted to find one on my own. I am capable of finding a girl whose heart I could win with no assistance from Mum or my sisters.

When my brothers and I reached adulthood, Mum mentioned that there was a girl in Aweil, South Sudan, that Aketch suggested to any of my brothers or me. The girl was Aketch's neighbor, and Aketch had known her for a long time. The girl, Nyibol, was recommended for any of us who might be interested to marry her in the near future. Mum mentioned Nyibol several times when the family ate dinner, but none of us took it seriously. When I went to South Sudan in 2016 to visit family, Nyibol showed up at my sister's house, and Aketch introduced her to me. The girl that I once heard about at the dinner table was now in front of me. She was a tall Dinka girl who stood at five feet, ten inches. She was twenty years old and was okay looking with big, white teeth and a slim body. When the girl returned to her house, I reminded my sister that I did not come to South Sudan to find a woman. I came to visit family members and was not interested in the girl.

I was frank and honest. I clearly told my sister that I already had a girl in mind. At that time, I had a plan to return to university to pursue a master's degree and then pursue a Luo girl named Achieng, whom I had started talking to in January 2015. Her uncle and I were good friends and served together in the US Army. Achieng was studying petroleum engineering in Malaysia, which I found intriguing. Although I told my sister the truth, she insisted that I get to know Nyibol. I asked my sister, "What is it about this Nyibol in particular?"

"She is a family-oriented girl who respects herself. She is the type of girl who values education, and she has a great reputation in the community. She has good manners and is trustworthy. She is someone who can be a great wife. Many men have come for her, including the former governor of Aweil state who later became the army general chief of staff, General Paul Malong Awan." After hearing what my sister had to say, I told her that I would get to know Nyibol, but my heart was not in it.

On my last few days in South Sudan, I met the parents of Achieng, whom I seriously wanted to pursue. Her father was very humble, calm, educated, quiet, and soft-spoken with a laid-back personality. He and I spoke briefly, but I spoke with respect and serious caution because he could potentially be my future father-in-law. Achieng's mother, whom I met several times via Facebook video and who was living in Malaysia to be near Achieng, happened to be visiting her husband in Juba, South Sudan. She was very friendly, confident, educated, and talkative. She recognized me right away when the opportunity for self-introduction came. I was happy that I got to meet both of Achieng's parents in person. My cousin whispered to me that it was a perfect time to propose to Achieng's parents right there since both of them were present. I refused and told him that I wanted to win the girl's heart on my own. I told my cousin that nowadays, in this new generation, it's better to know the girl first before you approach her parents. He agreed.

On May 10, 2016, I returned to the United States from the Republic of South Sudan, and my next trip was to Malaysia to see Achieng. I had told her that I would pay her a visit. The fact that I had met her parents gave me confidence, and I was ready to make an audacious move to go halfway around the world to see a girl whom I sincerely liked. I shared my plan with my family, and I told Achieng and her mother that I would visit in October. Achieng's mother told me that I was welcome anytime. My mother supported me and wished me safe travels.

Three weeks before my scheduled trip, Achieng had blocked my number. I thought that was rude but excused the behavior because I didn't feel I had enough information. It also didn't change my mind about courting her, so on October 2, 2016, I arrived at Kuala Lumpur International Airport and set foot in Southeast Asia for the first time.

Malaysia is a nation that occupies parts of the Malay Peninsula and the island of Borneo. The country is known for its beautiful beaches and rainforests, and its citizens are a mix of Malay, Chinese, and Indian. European cultural influence was also visible and hard to miss.

I was looking forward to seeing Achieng and her family. When I got to my hotel, I called Achieng's mum to let her know I arrived safely and that I would meet the family the next day. She was pleased and called Achieng to let her know that I had arrived. The next day, I got an Uber to Achieng's home.

"Welcome to Malaysia! You are a very brave young man and intelligent to know your way around the world," said Achieng's mother.

"Thank you, and it's great to see you again," I told her.

She warmly welcomed me to her home, and I met Achieng's younger brother who just arrived from school. The two of her brothers greeted me and were probably wondering who I was. Achieng's mother gave me some water to drink and told me to feel at home. I politely refused to drink water; in our culture, a man should not drink or eat at a house where he is interested in a girl. We chatted for a long time, and I enjoyed her conversation. She was a good chatter, and we spoke about many interesting things.

On the second day, Achieng welcomed me to Malaysia through a short conversation over the phone along with her younger sister. I was happy to hear from both of them and was looking forward to meeting them.

On my third day in Kuala Lumpur, the girl whom I crossed the Indian Ocean and other small islands to see finally showed up around 7 p.m. from her university three hours outside Kuala Lumpur. When she entered the living room, she kissed her mum on the cheeks and greeted her warmly. Then she came toward me, and I got up to greet her. I greeted her in the old-fashioned way by extending my right hand for a handshake. We did not speak much while we were around the family. Achieng was a light-skinned girl, and I was stunned by her natural beauty, height, voice, smile, and the dimple on her right cheek. She had a Luo traditional mark beside her left eye, which I was able to see when she was near me. I found the traditional marking very attractive! More than her physical beauty, I was attracted to her intelligence, which left me speechless. One thing I could not see was her heart. I could not tell if she was a good person or not. Knowing her heart was a big deal to me and would determine everything.

The opportunity to speak to her and hang out with her came when she, her brothers, and I went out. I discovered that she had a great sense of humor, which I loved. Like her mother, she was a talkative person, which made communication easy. Her brothers were her soldiers, and her family was near her heart. While we were out, I saw her answering and receiving text messages. It did not bother me at all because I wanted to observe.

At the time of my visit, Achieng and I were friends, but she knew that I wanted more than just friendship. I had told her before that I would steal her heart and take her breath away. She laughed and asked me, "Why are you so confident?" I told her, "If I want something, I go get it. I can win your heart." She never believed me. I came to Malaysia to show her that I was serious. She took it as a joke, but I was not playing. While I was in Malaysia, I did wonder if she was taken, but I never focused on that. I simply wanted to get an idea of what type of girl she was and to plan on how to win her. After four days, she returned to the university, and her brothers and I helped carry her things to her car. I got a hug, which I thought was nice because I did not expect it. Her mother watched us from the balcony.

When Achieng returned to the university, I visited a guy friend of mine who was studying in Malaysia. He was a relative of one of my good friends who lived in our community in North Carolina. While I was at my friend's house, he said, "Brother, I'm going to be honest with you. The girl you came to visit is dating this West African guy, but don't worry, he won't marry her. You will be her future husband. Keep talking to her, and you will eventually win her." I sincerely thanked my friend for his honesty and for being positive. He went on to say, "Her family are great people. Her dad is an awesome and humble man." My friend showed me some photos to serve as evidence of what he said. I looked at them and had nothing to say.

When I had the chance to speak with Achieng, I asked if she was in a serious relationship with the West African guy. She became fierce and said he was just a friend. I was not aware she was dating someone, but I remember her saying she had several people who were interested in her. I did not care who was interested in her or which country they came from because the best man would eventually win her, and I was confident in myself.

She never officially told me she had someone special. I told Achieng, "If you are dating him, then just be careful with him because West African guys tend not to be serious with South Sudanese girls." I gave her my sincere advice as someone who genuinely cared. My advice to her was based on my experience back in America of knowing West African guys and their relationships with South Sudanese-American girls. Achieng was offended and became angry at me. After I arrived and discovered she had someone, she told me I had no business finding things out about her life. The truth was, I did not search; the information was shared with me through a trusted friend who knew about her relationship, and I confirmed with her in a genuine way. My friend knew that I was genuinely interested in Achieng because I took the time to come so far. There was nothing offensive about my advice to her. I apologized to her for anything I said or did that she perceived as disrespectful. Deep down in my heart, I knew she took things out of context. She knew what she was doing. When I returned to the US, I left Achieng alone.

During the long period I was not talking to Achieng, I got to know Nyibol through phone conversations, but there was no chemistry. After I got to know her for several months, I began to see a pattern. Nyibol and her family always asked me for money to do this and that. She wanted money to purchase an iPhone, hair, shoes, clothes, and furniture. Her little sister asked for money for school fees and other things. It seemed to me that the entire family was after money. Nyibol's relationship with me seemed to be about money and opportunities she could have if the relationship developed into something serious. I strongly did not like this heavy reliance on me for financial gain or other opportunities. In addition, Nyibol was not mature enough by South Sudanese standards. Above all, she was stubborn and young.

Like most families in South Sudan, Nyibol's family fell below the poverty line. I knew from experience that poverty is a real thing and often forces young women to be married off for financial gain. The opportunities for the girl and her family were scarce, and I understood that fact. However, I knew that a relationship based solely on money would not work. Most girls in South Sudan desire South Sudanese men in the diaspora for opportunities and a chance to escape poverty. Most parents in South Sudan want their daughters to have opportunities they never had. Like most parents, Nyibol's parents hoped that if their daughter were married to someone like me who happened to live the USA, then it would benefit her and the family. It's partially true that South Sudanese men who live in the diaspora, such as the USA, Austria, Canada, and the United Kingdom, can pull girls out of poverty for better opportunities and a promise of a brighter future in the West.

In some cases, poor girls who married their way out of poverty manage to stay married and find more opportunity, and in other cases, it turns into a nightmare. The challenges in the West and the expectations are not exactly as most people would think. In general, girls and women in South Sudan think that those who live in the West have money and are living a comfortable life. This type of stereotype is completely false and overrated. Generally speaking, girls and women who marry a guy in the West to seek opportunities are unlikely to stay in the relationship. Half of those marriages are arranged based on opportunities to live in countries where quality of life, education, job opportunities, and basic services are better. I was never interested in an arranged marriage, and my mother would never support such a move for any of her children.

In June 2018, Nyibol and I both agreed to stop all communication. She did not like the idea, but I told her that it was the right thing to do. I had given her many chances to fix her habits, but nothing changed. I was not okay being in a relationship where everything was based on money and with someone I did not find on my own. Although I got to know her, there was still no chemistry, nor were we on the same page. Nyibol and I did not have many things in common, aside from the fact that her family and mine were from Aweil state. I saw Nyibol twice while I was in Aweil because I was occupied with family for whom I was truly there. In terms of education, Nyibol had a long way to go. She was still in high school at age twenty and needed time to grow. Based on where we were in life, we were incompatible in many ways.

Toward the end of 2017, I started talking to Achieng again in an attempt to win her. I strongly felt like she never gave me a chance or understood what I was trying to achieve with her while I was in Malaysia. Her mother understood that I was sincerely interested in her daughter. I respectfully asked her mother if she could speak to her daughter and let her know that I was serious about wanting her as a future wife. In December 2017, Achieng and I argued again because I asked her to stop being rude toward me because of her boyfriend. I honestly told her if she was still with him, then she just needed to be honest with me, and I wouldn't bother her. She did not confirm nor deny that she was still dating him, but I noticed a trend with her behavior. Whenever she was around her West African boyfriend, she would ignore my text messages and phone calls and push me away. When she was back to the university campus, she would be friendly again and show interest in me. I had enough of her games and stopped talking to her. She attempted several times to get my attention in 2018, but I ignored her. A whole year went by, and we never communicated.

Since June 2018, Achieng had been consistent with her attempts to start a conversation. She would text me once in a while and liked and commented on my Facebook photos, which I interpreted as signs of her wanting to come back to me. I was right, as she later revealed. In January 2019, we started to communicate once again. We talked for three to four hours on the phone and FaceTimed on other days. She was blown away to discover that I was still into her and wanted her to be my future wife. I was still blown away by her brilliant mind. By this time, she was twenty-eight years old and had completed her bachelor's degree. Her mother had passed, and she seemed to be looking forward in life. She told me that she had prayed about me and asked God for a sign to see if I was the one for her. Her prayer was actually answered, and that was why she was shocked to learn that I loved her all that time.

On February 2019, I put my uncle on a plane for the first time in his life to go to Juba, the capital of South Sudan. His mission was to go and ask for Achieng's hand from her father and her family on my behalf. My uncle was accompanied by his son and a village elder. This was another bold step that I took in the name of love.

"Son, do you truly love this girl?" my uncle asked me.

"I always wanted her with all my heart. There is no doubt here on my end, uncle," I replied.

"No worries, son. We will go and represent you well. I have experience with this type of mission," he said with incredible amount of confidence in his voice.

Before my uncle arrived in Juba, Achieng's father had called her to let her know that I was sending my uncle because I wanted her. Achieng accepted.

My uncle went to Juba and met with Achieng's father and family. I could not wait to hear about the result of the traditional marriage meeting. The next day, my uncle called and said, "It's all done. The family has accepted you with all their hearts." I was speechless and overwhelmed with joy. I was the happiest man on Earth because I finally won the hand of the woman I loved.

In April 2019, I made another audacious step and visited Achieng, this time not as a friend but as her future husband. In other words, she was traditionally engaged to me and was my fiancé. I arrived in Kuala Lumpur, Malaysia, and she was there to pick me up from the airport. Achieng surprised me with kisses and hugs, and that made the long trip even more worth it. The way she welcomed me marked a new chapter in our relationship. We had not seen each other in three years, and finally things seemed to be working out.

On my second day in Malaysia, we talked about expectations for the relationship. I told her that I loved her and said we needed to make our parents proud now that things were serious between us. I honestly told her that I was happy and could not wait to have her as my wife. I had one request for her: to have no further contact with her ex-boyfriend. "I am your future, and he was your past. He must remain in the past. I do not want another problem," I said. And she agreed. I respectfully asked her to block her West African ex-boyfriend from her phone and all social media right there in front of me. "I don't know how to do it," she said with smile that indicated discomfort. She eventually blocked the guy's phone number.

Fifteen minutes later, while she and I were getting ready to go out for dinner, her ex-boyfriend called her brother's phone. Her brother handed the phone to her, and I immediately knew who it was. "Stop being annoying. I don't like such people. I cannot talk to you," she told her ex in a raised voice. She did not mention his name since I was present. I got really upset, but I kept calm because her little brother was around.

While we were on our way to grab dinner, my heart was heavy with anger. I could not believe he was still in the picture. "Cool down. Cool down," she asked me several times. She knew I was not happy. I could barely eat when our dinner made it to our table. *Is this girl worth all the effort?* I asked myself. She had plenty of time to deal with her ex-boyfriend before I arrived in Malaysia, and what I saw was not acceptable at all. I trusted her when she told me that she was no longer with him since 2017. What I saw was completely the opposite of what I expected.

While I was in Malaysia, I did speak to her ex-boyfriend via WhatsApp video call. This was after I refused her offer for us to meet in person. I was not comfortable meeting a guy I had no interest in seeing. The video call revealed all the information I needed to know.

"This is Bol Maywal," said Achieng. "I told you about him. He is my fiancé from the USA. He is South Sudanese as well."

"How are you, brother?" I asked.

"I'm well," he replied, "And you?"

"I'm fine. Look, brother, I understand that you once dated her. Whatever you two had was the past. She is now my fiancé, and I need you to respect her decision. I want you stay away from her starting today."

"When did this all happen?" he asked.

Achieng jumped in, "It's none of your business."

"I always wanted her," I said. "And you were always in the way. I started talking to her in 2015, and I understand you dated her in 2016. Please stay away from her. You are now the past, and I am her future husband."

"Do you know her family? Does her family know you?" he asked.

"Yes, the family knows him," she said.

"All this time, where were you? You don't have someone in the USA?" he asked.

"All this time I wanted her," I said. "All I want you to do is to stay away from my girl."

"She is my friend," he said.

"You two cannot be friends. I do not want to argue with you over this friendship thing. I am her fiancé, and I don't want you around my future wife. I need you to understand this."

"He is the right person," Achieng said. "You lost me forever."

"Please take care of her," he said.

"Thank you for your advice," I responded. "Don't worry about that. It's my job to take care of her."

Finally, he asked, "Can you get me off the speaker? I want to say something in private."

I excused myself to give them a moment to speak privately. During our conversation, I could see that her ex-boyfriend was not happy. He was shaking his head in disbelief once he discovered that Achieng and I were engaged. I could see he still had strong feelings toward her and was emotionally broken. I have no idea what was said in their brief private conversation. It's clear that my fiancé had never told her ex-boyfriend she was engaged to me.

Two months after I returned to the United States, my fiancé still had not done what I asked of her. Her ex-boyfriend was still friends with her on Facebook, and she still had contact with him. Again, I asked her respectfully to get rid of him and said I wanted no contact in any way, shape, or form between them. This time, she asked, "Why? We are friends."

"You cannot be friends with someone whom you once dated, especially when we are in a serious relationship," I replied. Again, I gave her time to deal with her ex-boyfriend. In August, she brought up his name again and told me that the ex-boyfriend had helped her get her car fixed. I reminded her once again that I was not comfortable with her ex-boyfriend being around her.

On August 2019, I received a list of items for the dowry to marry Achieng. My family and I were honored to have reached this milestone in the relationship. My elder brother, uncle, and Mum sat down on the weekends to discuss the dowry list we received from our in-laws. The entire dowry was worth approximately $60,000. My elder brother and my mother suggested that my uncle in South Sudan should return to my in-laws and have the dowry amount reduced. I refused and told both of them that the girl was worth more than the bride price requested by her family. Since I did not have to pay the entire dowry at once, I accepted it. We discussed the amount of the dowry that needed to be taken to Achieng's family before the wedding in March. We agreed on twenty-five to thirty cows, and I would pay the rest slowly once she was my wife.

Achieng, her sister, friend, cousin, and I were all planning the wedding. Everything was going well for a March 2020 wedding date. I was staying up late arranging things with my side of the family in South Sudan to have part of the dowry taken to her family by October 25, 2019. Her K-1 fiancé visa was approved by September 2019 for her come to America after the wedding. I sent her a copy of the document for her record. Everything was heading in the right direction.

Toward the end of September 2019, Achieng brought up her ex-boyfriend's name again. I became very upset and told her that I was not comfortable with him being around her and did not want to hear his name ever again. My fiancé did not seem to take my concern seriously. Her unwillingness to get rid of him made me question her claim of not having any feelings toward him. She told me she wanted to be open about whom she dealt with and wanted to keep him as a "friend" because he was helpful to her family on numerous occasions. I said that I honestly appreciated all the help he provided to her family. However, he must distance himself from her for the sake of peace and out of respect for our pending marriage. My fiancé was stubborn and demanded that he must stay as a friend. I told her that it was not going to be possible because that would cause tension.

I wrote to the ex-boyfriend via Facebook and asked him once more time to distance himself from my future wife. I told him his behavior was causing serious tension between my fiancé and me and would eventually lead to a huge problem between her family and mine. He did not reply. Instead, he forwarded my message to her. An argument ensued, and she revealed to me that her father would have a heart attack he if discovered that her Nigerian boyfriend was the cause of our problem. This was a strong evidence that her parents never wanted him.

She was angry and said I had no right to choose who could be her friend and who could not. I said remaining friends with her ex-boyfriend crossed my personal boundaries in the relationship, especially since she seemed more concerned about his feelings than mine. She said he was her friend whether I liked it or not. I said she needed to make a choice about whom she wanted to be with.

Our families got involved since we could not come to common ground. My uncle returned to Juba in an attempt to solve the problem and move forward with the wedding as planned. It was worked out between the families, but the tension between Achieng and me was still high. In October, I spoke to Achieng's aunt who was representing Achieng's mother, and she described the situation as "shameful," and I discovered that Achieng's father was really upset. I was not going to back down on this ex-boyfriend issue. As far as I knew, he was the past, and I was the future.

Truth pays dividends, and digging hard for it helps with decision-making. During our heated arguments, I learned more about the seriousness of their relationship before I came along. The guy she claimed to be a "friend" was once engaged to her, and she wore his ring. Her family knew about it but played down the fact. In other words, he was not a boyfriend, nor a friend, but a former fiancé. In 2016, he had asked her mother for her hand. He was ready to go to Juba, South Sudan, but the girl's mother stopped him. He was Nigerian, a foreigner in the eyes of her South Sudanese parents, and they would not accept him. I was accepted with all their hearts because of my South Sudanese and Luo background, and I came in the right way to ask for their daughter's hand according to our tradition. My fiancé claimed she broke up with him in June 2017, but that does not seem to be true. If that were true, her former fiancé would not have shown such strong feelings toward her in April 2019 when he discovered that she was engaged to me.

I felt I had given Achieng 110 percent to the end. I never gave up on her when there were many reasons to do so. During the time I wanted to win her heart, I showed clarity, consistency, commitment, loyalty, honesty, respect, faithfulness, and above all, love. The situation had gotten to a level where elders and parents were disappointed, and I was the most disappointed.

To be fair to the girl who became my fiancé, she wanted to be with me to please her family, but I don't think her heart was ever with me, due to her former fiancé. Our relationship was in free fall because she still had feelings for the other guy, which she always denied. But if she never had feelings for him, getting rid of him would not have been a problem that could risk her marriage. She tried to blame me for putting our marriage at risk because I did not trust or listen to her. In my mind, I simply made my boundaries clear and remained firm.

While the situation between my fiancé and me became a major crisis, I thought about what Mum told us when we were still teenage boys: "Guys, look for respect from your future partners. Look for a woman who demonstrated respect to her parents and others. All men desire to be respected by their wives." I honestly did not see respect from my fiancé when she was dealing with me. She had more respect for her ex-boyfriend than for me. She had no respect for another gentleman who attempted to mediate between us. Although she was very attractive and educated, I never saw inner beauty in her. Instead of being gentle with me, she was fighting me and defending her ex-boyfriend while praising him in my face. My fiancé was not honest, loyal, gentle, respectful, or patient. Instead of fighting the problem together, she was fighting me and making unrealistic demands. She was the one who put herself between two men, demanding to keep both.

Like a soldier, I carefully chose my battles with my fiancé. The battle was asking her to get rid of her ex so that we could focus on the bigger things—our wedding and our future together. After almost three years of wanting her, I succeeded in getting her, but I did not succeed in keeping her. No man can keep a woman who does want to stay, especially if her heart is with someone else.

I did what I could to the best of my ability to win her. I traveled to another country for her and took her to one of the tallest and most famous buildings in Kuala Lumpur for dinner. I got on my knees to put a ring on her hand under a beautiful Sunset in Langkawi. I never expected her to be perfect. But I will never accept an ex-boyfriend or ex-fiancé to be put above me. It's all good to be in love with a woman whom my heart desires, but respect and dignity are something I cannot compromise. My relationship with Achieng was the closest I got to getting married to a woman I sincerely loved, yet it was the worst experience I ever had with a woman.

"Behind every strong man is an even stronger woman." I honestly believe in this saying. As a young leader in the United States Army and a future political leader, I want a strong woman behind me as I continue on the path of leadership. I want a partner who can value me as a man and display respect, loyalty, honesty, patience, gentleness, personal courage, and above all, unconditional love. I have chosen a leadership path where challenges will arise, and I need a partner who will hold me up on my worst days. Finding the right woman is not only about me, but also about my future children who deserve a wonderful mother. My mother's life exemplifies what a strong woman ought to be.

In all honesty, Achieng did not give her all, nor was she honest with me, her family, or her former fiancé. At the beginning, she gave her word to her family and me. Then she turned around and broke it. I am happy that I gave my all, and both families knew that. I do not regret pursuing her because I truly believed I wanted her in my life. I am the type of man who carries out a mission to the end. I'll take the lessons I learned from this relationship and move on to the next chapter in my life without regrets.

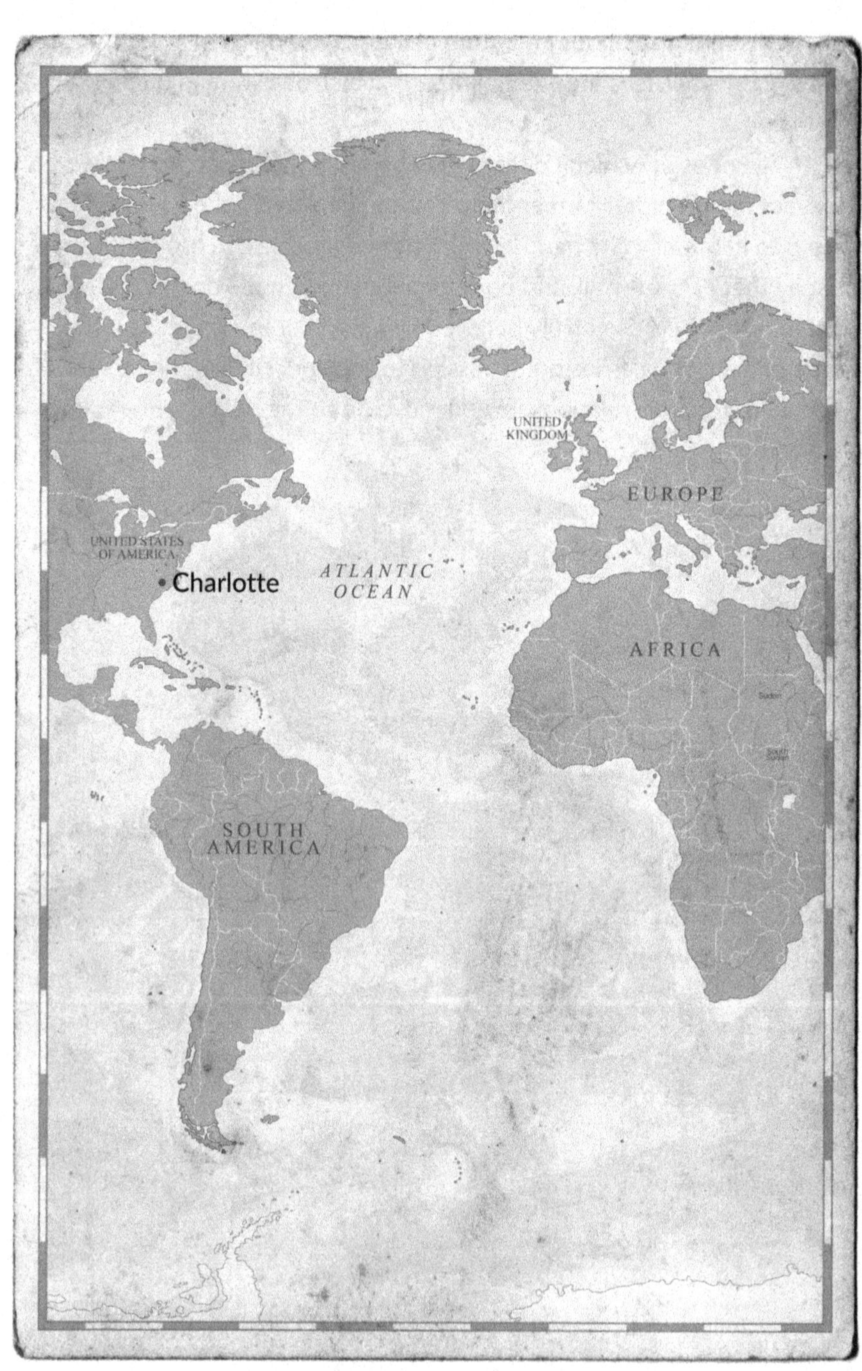

UNITED KINGDOM
EUROPE
UNITED STATES OF AMERICA
Charlotte
ATLANTIC OCEAN
AFRICA
Sudan
SOUTH AMERICA

CHAPTER 14

A Mother's Promise Fulfilled

**I will not violate my covenant or
alter what my lips have uttered.**

– Psalm 89:34 (NIV)

The best promises are made in difficult times. At the beginning of the Second Sudanese Civil War, my mother took her mother's advice and ran into the bush to escape the bloody war. Mum never looked back as her journey took her to northern Sudan, across into Egypt, and eventually to the US. Mum promised Grandma Abuk that she would take her children to safety and raise them well in a faraway land that was free from violence. My mother kept her promises to her mother and to her children on a remarkable journey that was filled with uncertainly.

As Nelson Mandela once said, "I learned that courage was not the absence of fear, but the triumph over it." It took an incredible amount of courage on my mother's part to keep her promises in the face of the numerous obstacles life threw at her. Throughout her journey, Mum demonstrated her commitment by enduring the sharp pains in life and refusing to let obstacles blur her vision for her children.

Currently, my mother has twenty-two grandchildren, eleven of them living in South Sudan, one in Egypt, and eleven born in the United States. The number of her grandchildren may increase in the future since my younger brothers and I are not yet married. It's my hope that one day these children will draw inspiration from their grandmother who struggled and persevered in life, as described in this book. Hopefully, they will learn that dreams are achievable and that promises ought to be kept despite difficulties.

Like most great parents, my mother has always seen far beyond what my siblings and I could see. When South Sudan became an independent country in 2011, Mum did something incredible and surprising. She sent money to my sister to purchase pieces of land for all her children in South Sudan, in addition to the land her family inherited from her father. Mum knew that once South Sudan stabilized, there would be land grabbing by the elite and wealthy, so she went ahead and had my sister secure land in case any of us wanted to return to South Sudan in the near future.

My mother's journey from Panjab village to Charlotte, North Carolina, had many firsts and many stories that will be told for generations in our family. Her story is of a poor, uneducated woman who fled a hostile country barefoot, alone with her children, and struggled to provide the best she could for her children. By keeping her promises, she succeeded in providing a safe place to live with educational opportunities for all. In the process, one child (that's me) succeeded in school all the way through completion of a master's degree and serving in the US Army as an officer, making her proud. It's true that refugee and immigrant stories have been told millions of times by others and are all part of the American story.

My mother was born just a generation past colonialism, a time when Africans were beginning to enjoy their independence from their colonial masters. She was part of the generation that did not allow girls to go to school. Looking back, I think about all that she's seen throughout her journey—the heartache of the First Sudanese Civil War, the pain of the second, the start of the liberation struggle that forced her brother to fight an oppressive regime, hardship in the displacement and refugee camps, and acclimation to a new life in the United States.

On July 9, 2011, my mother learned of the birth of a new country, the Republic of South Sudan, through a TV screen. This was a special and emotional moment. Her younger brother, Ungua, fought and sacrificed his youth and energy to help liberate southern Sudan. Although her brother struggles with PTSD today, she knows that his liberation struggle was worth it.

When Mum arrived in the United States with our family nineteen years ago, she had a permanent green card like most of our family members. All of us went on and took the US citizenship exam and became American citizens. Unlike most of us, Mum could neither read nor write, and that was an obstacle to her getting her citizenship. She had her permanent green card for eighteen years and would renew it periodically. But her unyielding desire to be an American citizen never ceased despite the language barrier and the challenges she faced as someone who never went to school as a young girl. She never gave up on her dream to be an American. She went to community college after work and studied hard. She took the test and failed several times, but still she never gave up. On October 21, 2019, my mother finally passed her US citizenship exam.

"Proud American at last! I am proud to be an American," she said proudly with a friendly smile in her face. This was a great achievement for someone whose story of courage and perseverance in pursuit of the American dream has finally become true. "I realized that I was part of what makes America great: its diversity and its acceptance of anyone who comes here in pursuit of the American dream," she told us. My mother left her family and everything to fulfill a promise, and America was that special place where her promise could be kept to her children and her dreams realized.

Our fellow Americans who were born on American soil sometimes take the responsibilities and privileges of being an

American citizen for granted. The truth is that immigrants and refugees have to work ten times as hard to earn US citizenship. During the swearing-in ceremony on November 5, Mum was happy to be in room full of people from various races, religions, and ethnicities. She said something that was quite remarkable: "Taking the ceremony oath for the first time in my life authenticated my feelings about how great America is. It made me feel proud to be a citizen of this nation that is a beacon of freedom, justice, peace, equality, and democracy."

We see that Mum is growing older. It's time for us to take care of her just as she has done for us. Her health has begun to trouble her sometimes, but she continues to fight on. Recently I asked my mother what her future dreams are for her grandchildren. She said, "I want all of them to know their culture and learn their grandmother is tough. This is a must because true sense of self starts by knowing yourself and your people. I wish them love among themselves and their relatives. I wish them courage to work out challenges that come with life. I wish them joy—in all things, there are brighter days ahead. I wish them strength, to stand tall for what they believe in. I wish them curiosity, always striving to learn and be educated people. I wish them prosperity and achieving it honorably. I wish them peace, love, and happiness. I wish them strength and self-confidence to follow their dreams." As she spoke confidently, I was moved by this blessing for all her current and future grandchildren.

My mother is the best mother any child could ask for. I'm grateful that she shaped my life to become the person that I am today. I know she wants me to return to her village to preserve the family legacy and bring peace and development, not only to her village but also to South Sudan as a whole. As far as the whole of South Sudan is concerned, I'll have to work with other like-minded young leaders to achieve that mission. The task of bringing electricity, running water, a school, roads, and a clinic or hospital to her village has been given to me. I will do my best to fulfill these ideals. Despite the numerous challenges that will come along the way, I will remember how Mum never gave up on her promises to her mother or to us. I promise her that I'll do my best, and I'll draw inspiration from her great example of perseverance.

Left to right: Adout Goi Ungua, Rebecca, Moses Goi, and baby Goi in Matthews, North Carolina.

Children of Adout Goi Ungua

Ayuot (daughter)
born in 1974, died of natural causes, and buried in Panjab village

Aketch (daughter)
born in 1978 in Arum-makar village, southern Sudan

Achalla (daughter)
born in 1980, died of natural causes, and buried in Panjab village

Akol (daughter)
born in unknown year, died of natural causes immediately
after birth, and buried in Panjab village

Allah-jabo (son)
born in 1983 in Panjab village, toddler
when our mother fled her village

Amal (daughter)
born in 1985 in Muglad, Sudan

Maywal (son)
born in 1988 in Muglad, Sudan

Bol (son and the author of this book)
also known as Uchu, born in 1989 in El-Haj Yousif, Sudan

Amoe (son)
born in 1992 in Al-Shijra, Sudan

Makot (son)
born in 1995 in Khartoum, Sudan

Works Cited

Apai, Gabriel (2007). *Our Inheritance for New Horizons: Sudanese Luo Traditional Culture:* Queensland: TAFE Queensland.

Crump S. (2014). *Taxi Company Owner Says He Was Shut Out of Process.* https://www.wbtv.com/story/25158023/taxi-company-owner-says-he-was-shut-out-of-process/ Accessed 10 April 2014.

CNN (2019). *September 11 Terror Attacks Fast Facts.* https://www.cnn.com/2013/07/27/us/september-11-anniversary-fast-facts/index.html/Accessed 23 March 2020.

CBS News (2014). *Charlotte Mayor Patrick Cannon Resigns After His Arrest on Corruption Charges.* https://www.cbsnews.com/news/charlotte-mayor-patrick-cannon-arrested-faces-corruption-charges/ Accessed 10 April 2014.

Human Rights Watch/Africa (1994). Sudan "In the Name of God": Repression Continues in Northern Sudan. *Human Rights Watch / Africa* 6(9).

LT Col. Buentello, Gilbert (2015). *Kosovo Children Visit Bondsteel for Christmas.* Defense Visual Information Distribution Service. https://www.dvidshub.net/image/2344094/kosovo-children-visit-bondsteel-christmas/ Accessed 19 December 2015.

Ryan O. (2007). *Door of No Return Opens up Ghana's Slave Past.* https://www.reuters.com/article/us-slavery-ghana/door-of-no-return-opens-up-ghanas-slave-past-idUSL2121456420070320/ Accessed.18 July 2017.

Rolandsen, O. H. (2015). Another Civil War in South Sudan: The Failure of Guerrilla Government? *Journal of Eastern Africa Studies* 9(1), 163-174.

UNHCR (1951). *What is a Refugee?* The United Nations Refugee Agency. https://www.unhcr.org/afr/what-is-a-refugee.html/ Accessed 15 January 2018.

WBTV (2008). *Myers Park Ranked 38th Best High School in America.* https://www.wbtv.com/story/8348913/myers-park-ranked-38th-best-high-school-in-america/ Accessed 11 July 2017.

About the Author

Bol Maywal is a US citizen born in the middle of the Second Sudanese Civil War in a displacement camp in El Haj Yousif, Sudan. The war erupted in 1983 and officially ended in 2005. In 1997, Bol and his family fled Sudan and lived in a United Nations (UN) refugee camp in Egypt for several years. In 2001, Bol and family came to the US with assistance from the United Nations and Catholic Social Services, now called Catholic Charities. He entered elementary school unable to speak English and faced challenges as a refugee integrating into the local community. He persevered and earned his US citizenship on April 24, 2009.

From these life experiences, Bol has dedicated himself to serving others. He is a peace scholar, a former NATO Peacemaker, and a US Army officer. He worked briefly as a case coordinator for the Catholic Charities refugee resettlement office. Bol hopes to be a proactive global peacebuilder.

In 2013, Bol earned his bachelor's degree from Belmont Abbey College on an Army ROTC Scholarship, majoring in political science and minoring in military science. In 2015, as an officer in the US Army, he volunteered for a NATO Peace Operation Mission in Kosovo and was awarded a Non-Article 5 NATO Peace Medal in the service of peace and freedom. In early 2016, Bol was nominated by District 7680 as a candidate for a Rotary Peace Fellowship to study peace, conflict, and development at the University of Bradford in the United Kingdom. He graduated in 2019 with his master's degree and was named a Paul Harris Fellow.

Bol is the author of *A Mother's Promise: A Civil War Survivor and Her Pursuit of the American Dream*, a special tribute to his mother who raised him to be the leader he is today. He hopes the book can serve as an example to other young men and provide encouragement to widows, single mothers, and mothers to be the best versions of themselves to their children. He hopes this book can shed a positive light on refugees and immigrants and their contributions to America.

Bol believes that his mother's sacrifices contributed greatly to his success in life, and he is as proud of her as she is of him. Bol held numerous leadership positions to include deputy company commander with a unit in Georgia, United States. Bol hopes to go into politics, and he is determined to make a difference as a servant leader.

To invite Bol Maywal to be a guest speaker for your organization, contact him via his website or social media.

 BolMaywal.com

   BolMaywal

Major Willie Douglas administers the oath of office to Second Lieutenant Bol Maywal at the UNC Charlotte Army ROTC Commissioning Ceremony at Center City UNC Charlotte on May 10, 2013. *Photo courtesy of Mr. Curtis Lawrence, UNC Charlotte Army ROTC Staff.*

Mediterranean Sea
Sahara
AFRICA
South
Sudan
ECUATOR

Dear Reader,

My mother's life journey and my experience as a child has enabled me to wear many hats. I am a former refugee from Sudan, a former Rotary Peace Fellow, a former NATO peacekeeper, a US Army officer, a feminist, an inspiration, a proponent of education, a global citizen for peace, and a proud citizen of the United States.

My fellow Americans, let's continue to warmly welcome refugees and provide homes to those who seek peace, security, and hope, like my family did nineteen years ago. I believe we can stay true to our American values and our way of life without jeopardizing our national security. I believe every refugee who enters America must go through screening and vetting, just like my family did before we arrived in America. America's enemies must be prevented from using refugee status as a safe channel to do harm to American people.

To all the girls and women, I am on your team. Not just for now, but all the way. Let's continue to fight injustice and discrimination against girls and women domestically and internationally. Let's wage a war to end child marriages and all sorts of violence against women wherever it may be.

When it came to my education, it was a woman who was deprived of her education who served as a source of motivation for me to win scholarships. Let's support girls' and women's educations and leave nobody behind. When a woman is educated, she can extend her influence beyond her family, community, and nation.

As someone who was born in the middle of civil war, my mother's firsthand experience with war enabled me to always cherish peace. Peace benefits humankind regardless of their race, religion, gender, sexual orientation, and national origin. To seek peace, we ought to continuously plant seeds of peace in our families, communities, villages, nations, and along international borders. These seeds will grow into an army of peacekeepers. It is then can we truly know that we have planted something that is worth safeguarding to sustain us and our future generations.

We are our brothers' and sisters' keepers. Join a cause and contribute to making the world a little better than you found it. Let's do this!

Sincerely,
Bol Maywal